IN MEMORY
OF THE MICHELIN WORKMEN AND EMPLOYEES
WHO DIED GLORIOUSLY FOR THEIR COUNTRY.

ARRAS

LENS - DOUAI

AND

THE BATTLES OF ARTOIS.

" Proud and valorous City, previously the witness of many fierce strifes... For more than four years bore with admirable fortitude the horrors of the unprecedented battle fought at her gates. Ruined and almost annihilated, did not despair, but as soon as delivered, set to work again with admirable ardour. "

Légion d'Honneur and Croix de Guerre.

Naval & Military Press

THE OPERATIONS

From 1914

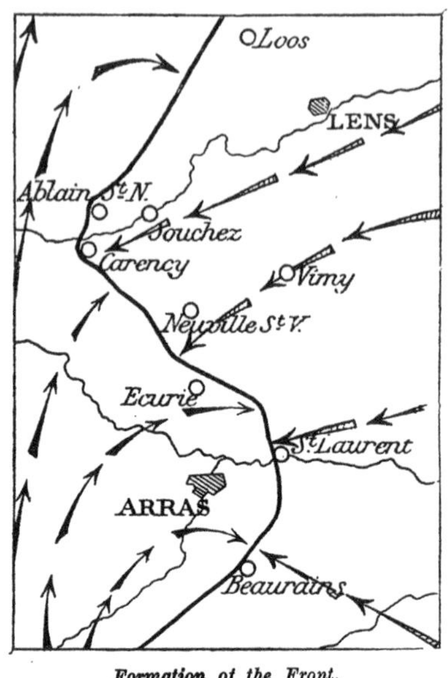

Formation of the Front.
OCTOBER 1914.

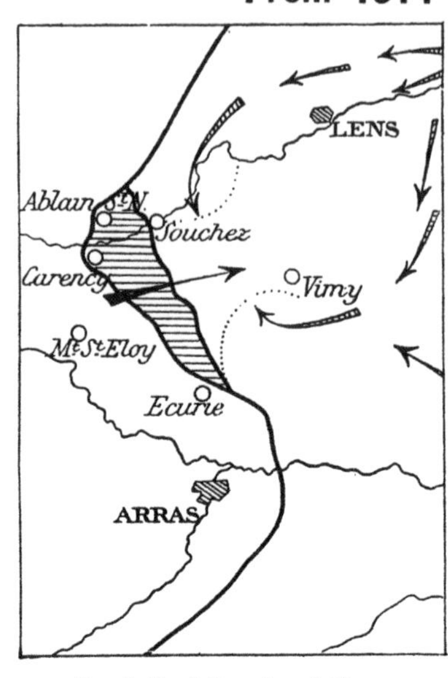

French Break-through and Enemy Counter-attack, MAY 1915.

In 1917

British Offensive, APRIL 1917.

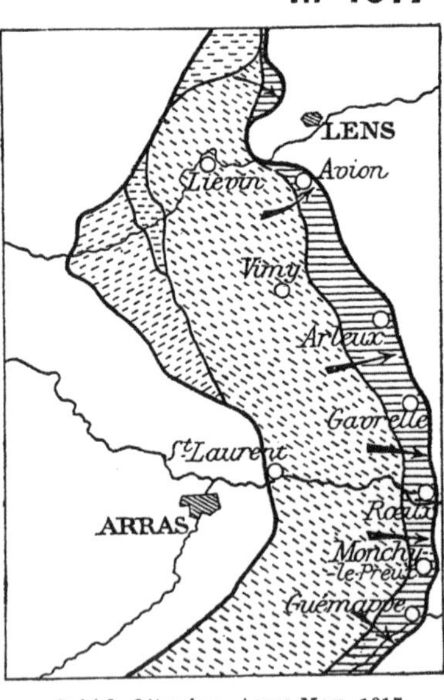

British Offensives, APRIL-MAY 1917.

AROUND ARRAS.

to 1916.

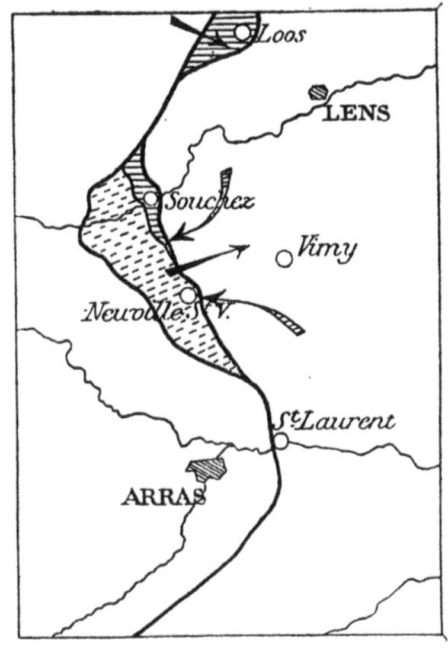

Franco-British Offensive, SEPT. 1915.

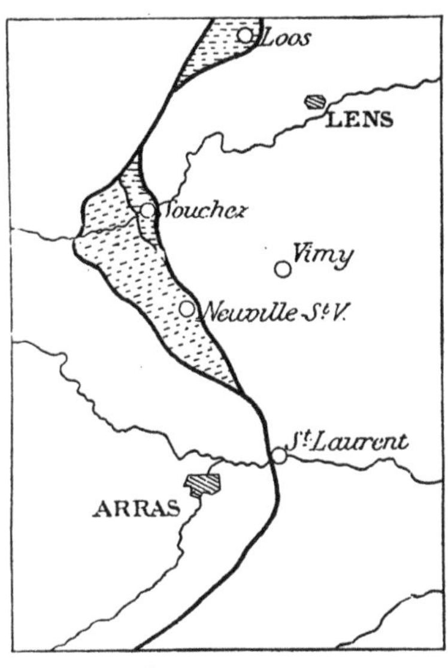

1916. *Situation unchanged.*

and 1918.

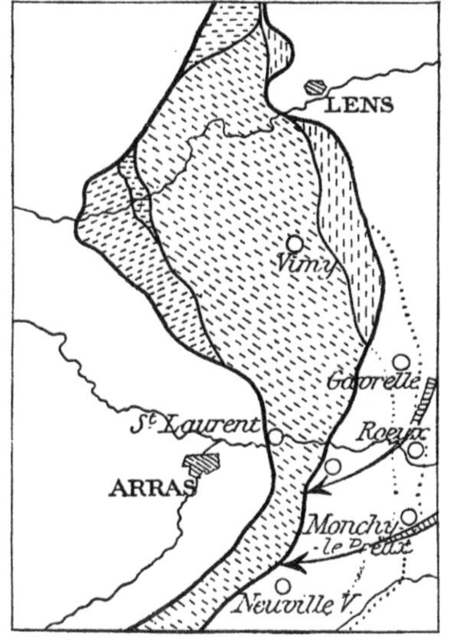

German Offensive, MARCH 1918.

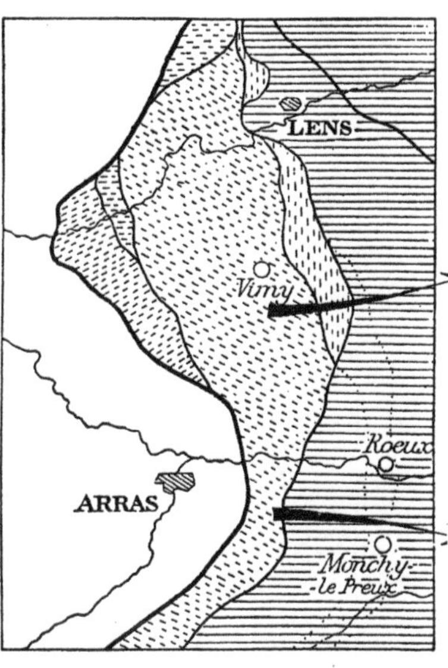

Victory Offensives, SEPTEMBER 1918.

THE RACE TO THE SEA AND THE FORMATION OF THE FRONT (1914).

About the middle of August 1914, when the French began their offensive in Belgium, General d'Amade, in command of a group of territorial divisions, took up his head-quarters at Arras. After the check at Charleroi, these divisions fell back (August 27) to the south-west, on the left of the retreating French Armies.

Light enemy forces entered Arras on September 6, withdrawing on the 9th, after requisitioning large quantities of stores.

After the Battle of the Marne, the forces under General d'Amade left Amiens for Arras, the auxiliary corps of light cavalry ("*spahis*") driving out the German cavalry patrols.

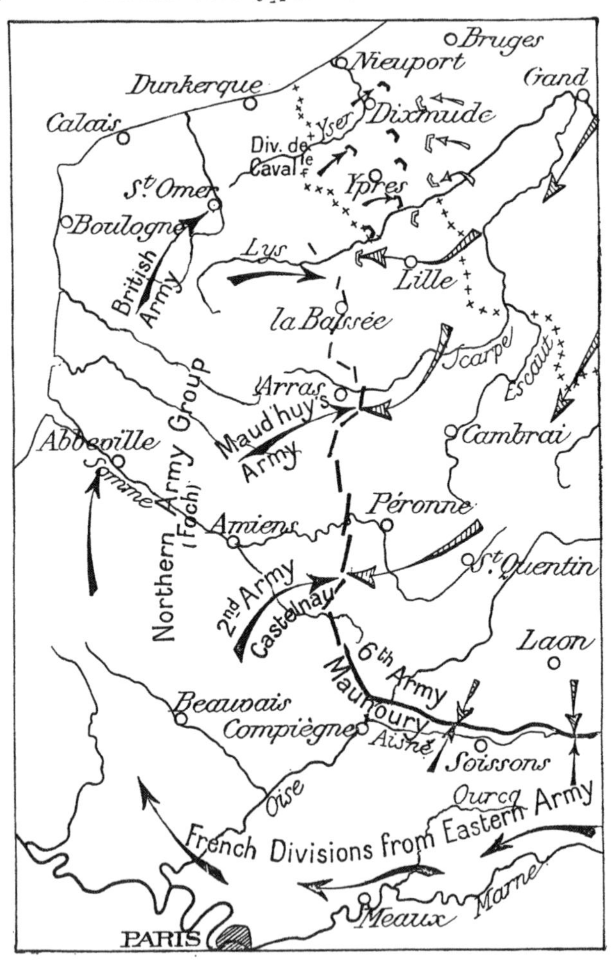

THE RACE TO THE SEA. (*See the Michelin Guide : The Yser and the Belgian Coast*).

General Maistre.

General Fayolle.

The enemy sought to outflank the French left, in order to force a decision, but the rapidity of the manœuvre carried out by General Foch parried the danger. The scene of action moved northwards, from the banks of the Aisne, and developed into the " Race to the Sea ", described in the Guide : " The Yser and the Belgian Coast ".

To the north-east of Arras, the Germans, thanks to their strong reserves, gradually drove back the light forces of the 1st Cavalry Corps.

General d'Urbal.

General de Maud'huy.

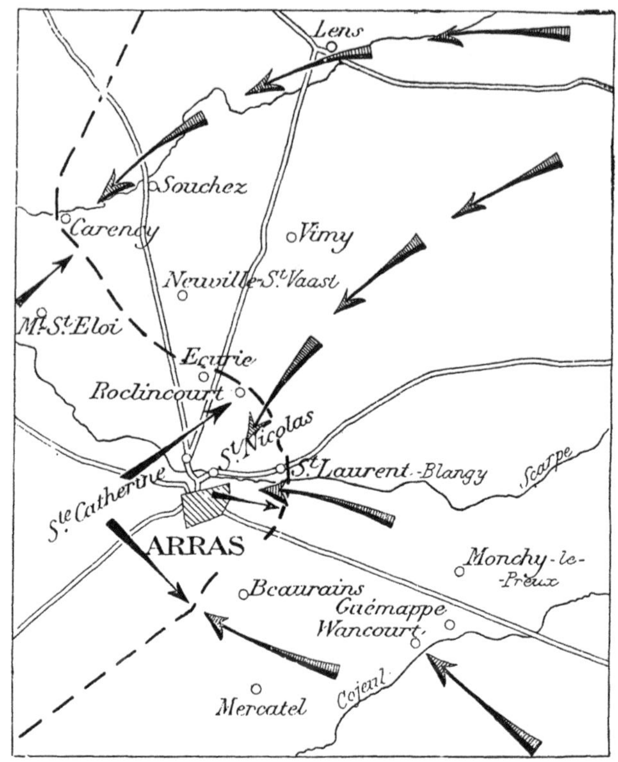

ATTACKS ON ARRAS (October 1914). FORMATION OF THE FRONT.

A number of French brigades and divisions arrived from the east. On September 30, the Alpine Division (General Barbot) detrained at Arras, and the next day held large enemy forces in check on the Cojeul Stream, and on the high ground near Monchy-le-Preux.

Guémappe, Wancourt and Monchy-le-Preux were already occupied, when the enemy attacked. Spread over a very wide front, the Alpine Division was gradually forced back, finally coming to a stand on positions facing east, where they held the Germans until the arrival of the 10th Corps (General de Maud'huy).

On October 3-4, the enemy renewed their attacks on Beaurains, Mercatel and the suburbs of Arras (St. Laurent-Blangy and St. Nicolas) with increased violence, but the Alpine Division stubbornly resisted.

Held in the centre, the enemy progressed northwards. On October 4, they entered Lens, defended only by a group of cyclists and an unmounted brigade of the 5th Cavalry Division. After taking Souchez and Neuville-St-Vaast, the Germans gained a footing on the ridge of Notre-Dame-de-Lorette. Turning Arras from the north, they attempted to reach the Scarpe, in order to crush the division under General Fayolle. The situation was critical, but the 10th Corps held the enemy, whose efforts now began to weaken.

In the Arras salient, the Alpine Division, exhausted and reduced to one-quarter of its full strength, was ordered to fall back upon a narrower front and to line up with the forces on the left and right. However, General Barbot refused to evacuate Arras, and the town was thus saved.

In face of such obstinate resistance, the enemy suspended their efforts for two weeks, pending the arrival of their heavy artillery, with which to lay siege to the town.

The bombardment began on October 21. In possession of the heights around the town, the Germans deluged the latter with shells. The huge 11in. and 8in. shells crushed the city and its artistic treasures. The beautiful watch-tower fell down on the 22nd, and the fires spread to the suburbs.

In the afternoon of the 22nd, under the eyes of the Kaiser, the Germans attacked the ruins of St. Laurent, whose burning houses collapsed amid the shells. Chasseurs, reinforced by Zouaves and sappers, who had just detrained, made a desperate resistance. Attacks and counter-attacks succeeded one another amid an inferno of fire, smoke and explosions.

Still the Alpine Division held on, their heroism being rewarded the next day, when the town, hard pressed from the north-east, was relieved by six battalions of Senegalese troops, which had been rushed up to the rescue. Thus a second time, Arras escaped capture by the enemy.

Unable to open up a way, the Germans turned their costly and unsuccessful efforts northwards, in front of Ypres and along the Yser.

Both sides dug themselves in, in the clay soil of Artois, and the respective lines gradually became defined. These organisations were of a most rudimentary character. To lie under canvas, or a sheet of corrugated iron was the fortune of the privileged few. Under the action of the rain, the clay sides of the trenches fell in, filling the latter with deep, sticky mud.

On both sides, the wire entanglements and *chevaux-de-frise* increased in depth. The Germans worked with great thoroughness, gradually transforming the villages into veritable fortresses, and hemming in the town with a formidable barrier.

The 33rd Corps (Pétain) and the 21st Corps (Maistre) of the 10th Army (d'Urbal) were holding this sector (*see sketch*, p. 8), the 33rd Corps occupying the trenches between Arras and Ablain-St-Nazaire, and the 21st, the lines between this village and Calonne Trench (1 km. north-west of Liévin).

The fighting was characterised by desultory gun and rifle fire, whilst occasionally, sharp fusillades spread like trains of powder along the lines, only to die down again. From time to time, daring raids were carried out under cover of the fog, but the main battle was being delivered in Flanders.

In December, battalions of the 21st Corps attacked the northern and western outskirts of Carency, but after making some progress they were held by the enemy's concentrated machine-gun fire. Throughout the winter, this sector was the scene of mine warfare and raids.

On March 15, the 153rd Infantry Regiment (21st Corps) made some progress along the northern edge of the Spur of Notre-Dame-de-Lorette, as the result of a series of spirited assaults.

This long, armed vigil in the mud, with its attendant local fighting, was, however, but the precursor of the coming great struggle of the Spring and Summer of 1915.

THE FRENCH OFFENSIVES OF 1915.

The attack of May-June — Conditions of the Attack.

Taking in the villages of Carency and Ablain-St-Nazaire, the German lines formed a dangerous salient. The enemy held all the high ground : the Notre-Dame-de-Lorette Spur, Vimy Ridge and Monchy-le-Preux Hill. Thus dominated, Arras and the whole of thc French lines were crushed beneath the fire of the German batteries, which were masked in the *corons* of Liévin and Angres, and in the smah woods behind Vimy Ridge.

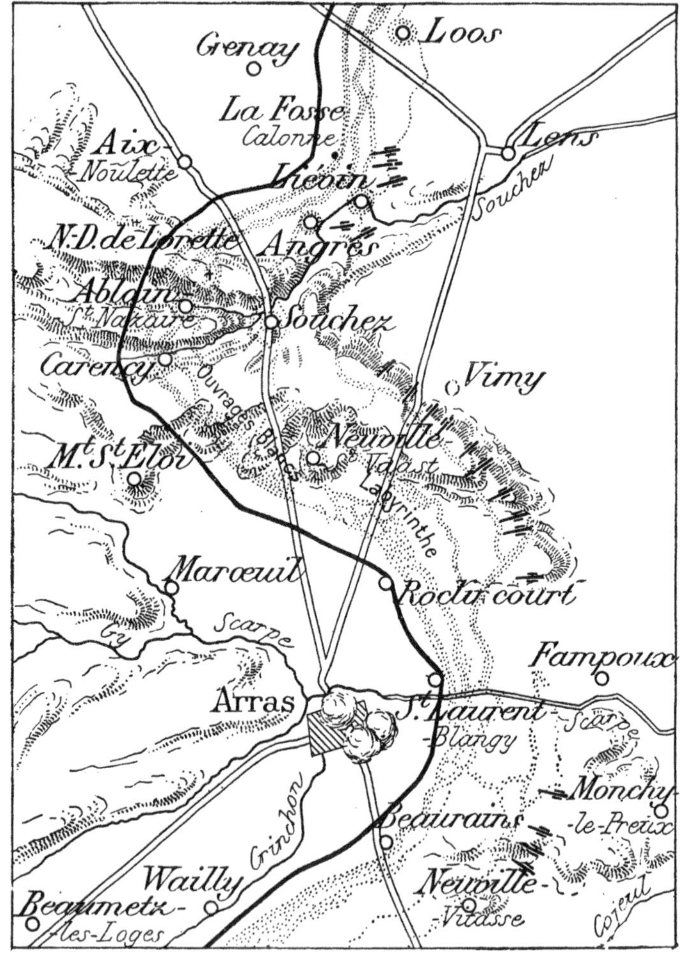

THE GERMAN LINES AROUND ARRAS.

In the Spring of 1915, the French G. H. Q. decided to relieve the pressure on Arras by carrying the heights which dominate the town to the north and north-east. The possession of these natural observation-posts and departure base would then enable the French, with the open plain of Lens and Douai stretching before them, to advance on those two important mining centres and railway junctions.

General Foch, commanding the Army Group of the North, was in charge of this offensive.

Under his direction, which adapted itself to the new tactical conditions of the battle, method took the place of improvisation. Each unit had its own special mission assigned to it ; the action of the artillery was clearly defined.

The front of attack was so equipped that the assaulting troops found themselves in front of their objectives. (The plan of attack was so well contrived that it was used as a model for several later offensives).

The means of action at the disposal of General Foch being limited, he decided to attack along a narrow front only (about six miles wide) from a point east of Roclincourt to the region of Notre-Dame-de-Lorette. In this zone were assembled powerful artillery and five army corps of veteran troops, including two of three divisions each.

The 21st, 33rd, 20th, 17th and 10th Corps were echeloned from Arras to the slopes of Notre-Dame-de-Lorette, being supported on the north by the 9th Corps opposite Loos.

The German positions, constantly consolidated since the fixing of the front line, were truly formidable. Unbroken lines of trenches, redoubts and *boyaux* extended all along the slopes of the heights to be conquered, whilst at the foot of the latter, facing the first French lines, ran a series of powerfully organised strong points, consisting of villages transformed into fortresses (Ablain-St-Nazaire, Carency, Neuville-St-Vaast, etc.), and newly constructed centres of resistance like the *Ouvrages Blancs* and *Labyrinth.*

The houses of each village were fortified and connected with one another, either by underground passages, from cellar to cellar, or by screneed paths. The cellars were propped and protected with armour, their vaulting being covered with a thick layer of concrete or sacks of earth. Loop-holes for machine-guns were pierced in the walls. The sub-basements of the enclosing walls, and the hedges, concealed trenches, which were protected by auxiliary defences (wire-entanglements, chevaux-de-frise, hedgehogs, etc).

The fortifications, like the *Labyrinth*, consisted of networks of trenches and deep *boyaux*, with underground shelters armed with numerous machine-guns. These shelters intersected one another in all directions, forming an inextricable maze. A number of flanking works and deep lines of barbed-wire everywhere protected the approaches.

However, these formidable defences in no wise dismayed the French. It was their first grand offensive, destined to carry them, they believed, within twenty-four hours, first to Douai, then to the frontier. At lasts they were to get out of the horrible trench mud, and under the May skies, fight their way in the open to Victory. Unbounded enthusiasm animated them, men and officers alike.

The Attack.

On May 9, 1915, after a violent artillery preparation with 75's and 155's, lasting several hours, the 10th Army attacked.

In the centre, the advance was extremely rapid. Starting from Berthonval Wood, regiments of the 33rd Corps (Pétain) captured the *Ouvrages Blancs* and the Arras-Béthune road (N. 37), as far as the outskirts of Souchez, then scaled the slopes of Vimy Ridge, reaching the upper crest. The enemy were taken completely by surprise, and either surrendered or hastily retreated.

The German front was virtually pierced. The panic spread as far as the suburbs of Lille, and the staff of the German IVth Army (Prince Rupprecht of Bavaria) began to remove their quarters. The advance here had exceeded the most sanguine expectations... Unfortunately, the attacking troops had gone forward too quickly in their excitement, and were now exhausted. Unprepared for this rapid advance (4 ½ kilometres in an hour), the French Commandment were unable to bring up the necessary reinforcements in time. Recovering from their surprise, the Germans rushed up their reserves in lorries and stopped the all too narrow gap in their lines.

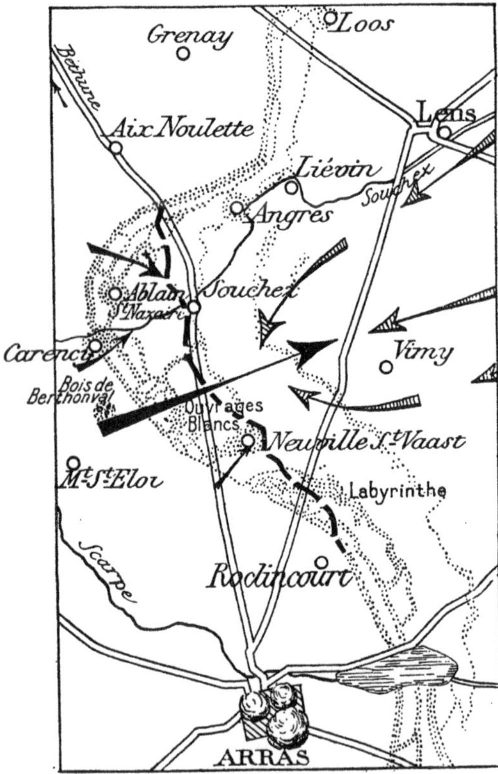

THE FRENCH ATTACK OF MAY 1915.
The advance was less rapid on the wings than in the Centre, thereby facilitating the enemy's counter-attacks.

To the left and right of the central attack the advance was much slower, the enemy's resistance being extremely desperate.

Although the German positions were deluged with hundreds of thousands of shells, the French were only able to conquer them by degrees, after bitterly disputed engagements lasting several days.

On the left, the attack against the famous hill of Notre-Dame-de-Lorette had begun long before the offensive of May 1915 (*See p. 71, for particulars of this action*). In December 1914, and again in March and April 1915, the 21st Corps (Maistre) had successively captured the three spurs which flank the south and south-western edge of the *massif*.

In May, they finally succeeded in reaching the summit of the plateau, and on the 12th, after four days of the fiercest fighting, captured the chapel of Notre-Dame-de-Lorette, which formed the key of the entire position. However, it was only on May 22 that the Germans were finally driven from the south-western slopes of the hill.

The capture of Carency was only completed on May 12, after having been entirely surrounded by General Fayolle's Division (33rd Corps).

The northern part of Ablain-St-Nazaire was occupied only on May 29. On June 1, after three days of violent fighting, with varying fortune, the sugar refinery, situated half-way between Ablain and Souchez, was finally captured. During these three weeks of fighting (May 9 to June 1), General Fayolle's division took 3,100 prisoners and buried 2,600 German dead, whilst their own losses in killed, missing and wounded, amounted only to 3,200.

At Neuville-St-Vaast, the conquest of the northern part of the village was only completed on June 9, after desperate fighting in the streets and houses. In the Labyrinth, where a footing had been gained as early as May 9, the struggle continued uninterruptedly until the middle of June, on the 17th of which month the entire position was taken.

By June 19, the offensive in Artois, begun on May 9, could be considered at an end. The fighting, although still very fierce, was merely intended to consolidate the conquered ground. It gradually degenerated into trench engagements, in which grenades and bombs played the main part. Through lack of reserves, and also owing to the narrowness of the front of attack, which did not allow of the break-through being promptly and fully taken advantage of, the offensive did not give the expected results, the advance being only from two to four kilometres. On the other hand, to keep the debouching positions of the Northern Plain, the Germans had been forced to engage sixteen divisions (over 300,000 men), and had suffered much heavier losses than the French. They, moreover, lost some 8,000 unwounded prisoners, 20 guns and about a hundred machine-guns.

A Great Leader.

In May 1915, the 33rd Corps, commanded by General Pétain, pierced the German Front.

Trench warfare, with all its attendant horrors, began again. The new lines were gradually consolidated in the shell-torn ground, the deep, foul mud of which swallowed up everything. Often, the trenches were mere ditches, whose sides were kept from falling in by thousands of sacks of earth.

The first lines passed through hideous places :

" Countless dead lay buried in the parapets of the trenches, dug in the thick of the battle during May. At every step, protruding through the wall, one saw here a hand or foot, there a tuft of hair or a piece of a tunic. Corpses on every hand... We were living among the dead.

" They lay rotting on the *bled* between the trenches, in front of the trenches, in the shell-holes, behind the sand-bags, everywhere. In those hot summer days their stench filled the air, drawing myriads of large black and green flies which settled in swarms everywhere, on everything.

" Yet in spite of the stench, the hot sun, the flies and the pitiless thirst, the men never flinched or allowed weariness or discouragement to get the better of them. The presence of these same dead, their comrades, steeled them to fight on.

" Dark but great days these, a symbol to those who lived through them of the horror and grandeur of this siege warfare. "

(Captain HUMBERT's " La Division Barbot ".

The Offensive of September 1915.

In September 1915, a fresh attack was launched against the Artois front, in combination with an offensive which was timed to take place simultaneously in Champagne, and whose chief object was to relieve the Russian front, where the Austro-Germans, during the Spring

BARRICADE AT NEUVILLE-SAINT-VAAST, IN MAY 1915.
This barricade separated the Allies' lines from those of the enemy.

and Summer of 1915 had conquered Galicia and Poland, and penetrated into Russia, as far as Brest-Litowsk.

This offensive, which was launched on the 25th, had been worked out several months previously at General Headquarters, in accordance with the methods of attack used in Artois, but arranging for all gains to be fully exploited.

The British, in liaison with the French 10th Army, attacked the German trenches near Loos, in the direction of Lens. The 10th Army, still under the orders of General d'Urbal, had for its objective the conquest of Vimy Ridge, that long spur which dominates the Plain of Douai.

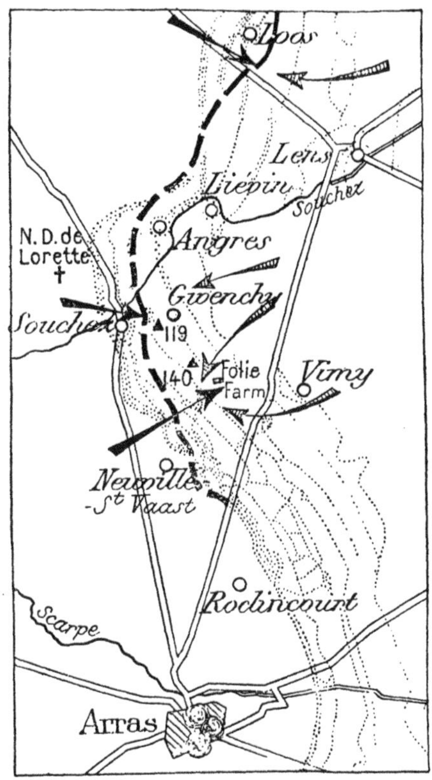

Franco-British Attack in Artois (September 1915.). *While the British attacked to the north, towards Lens, the French objective was Vimy Ridge.*

On September 25, at 12.30 p. m., after an artillery preparation lasting five days, the 33rd. Corps, under General Fayolle, who had succeeded General Pétain, captured the German trenches protecting the western outskirts of Souchez, and after carrying the park and Château of Carleul, attacked the village. However, the enemy offered such a desperate resistance that Souchez was only conquered in its entirety on the following day.

Other units, advancing simultaneously along the slopes of Vimy Ridge, carried three successive lines of trenches. On September 27-28, after desperate fighting, they captured Hill 119, east of Souchez, and advancing as far as the orchards of La Folie Farm, reached Hill 140, i. e. the culminating point of the crest. However, important enemy reinforcements, brought up from Lille, Valenciennes and Douai, stayed further progress, whilst the countless heavy guns which accompanied them, pounded the entire battlefield with terrific shell fire. (*See description of the battle on p.* 88).

The attack was thus brought to a stand, and soon the enemy's massed counter-attacks compelled the French to abandon the conquered ground on the Vimy Plateau. 2,600 prisoners, 9 guns, and a large number of machine-guns were captured by the French.

Trench warfare began again in October, the 8in. shells and large calibre "Minen" churning up the clay soil, until the entire sector was one vast bog. The works which had been laboriously carried out to protect the trenches from the encroaching mud, crumbled away under the bombardment. Further fighting became impossible during this, the " black period ", in the Artois Battle.

There was no protecting one's self against the mud, that formidable insistent foe.

In his book, *La Division Barbot*, Captain HUMBERT paints a striking picture of it :

...Let us take a look at this Alpine Chasseur, about to go up a communication trench.

The lower part of his body, up to his waist, is covered with his blue overalls, into which he has tucked the flaps of his tunic, supposing he has not cut them off. His legs, up to the knees, are tied up in sand-bags. Another sand-bag covers his helmet, which, in the moonlight, would otherwise draw the enemy's fire. He does not carry any blanket, as it would quickly become soaked with mud, so as to be useless. His only comfort is his tent cover which he has wrapped round his body. A bit of cloth is tied round the muzzle of his rifle, whilst the steel parts of the breech are protected with canvas, so that he may be ready to fire on reaching his post.

Two bulky haversacks and a two-litre water-bottle slung over his shoulders, help still further to weigh him down, as he enters the trench.

Sinking up to his knees, he tries to lift one leg out, but the heavy, sticky mud has closed over his foot. What is there to hold on to? Both sides of the trench have fallen in, and his hands grasp mud. However, he succeeds in moving a leg, but the muscles of his hip have to work hard, and after advancing a few yards he stops exhausted to recover his breath. Then he starts again. The bombardment begins. The 8in. shells come with a roar, the torpedoes without a sound. What is he to do? Lie down? he cannot, being stuck in the mud. Run, advance, retreat? He could not move more slowly than he does. Take cover? There is none whatever in the long, straight trench. He can only remain where he is, stuck fast in the mud ...

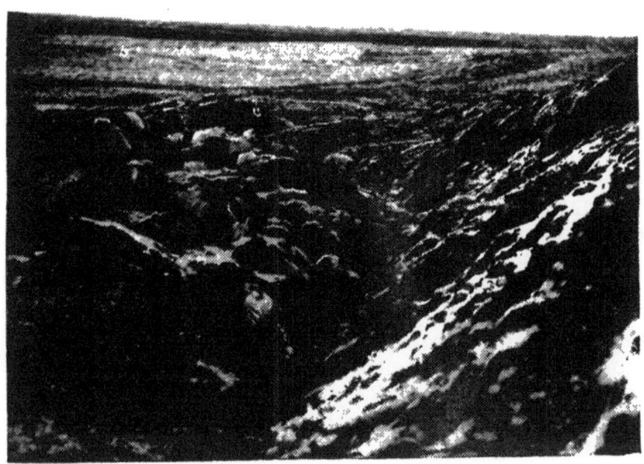

TRENCHES IN FRONT OF SOUCHEZ.

THE BRITISH OFFENSIVES OF 1917.

Relief of Arras.

From October 1915 to April 1917, no important attacks took place in the Arras sector.

The British extended their front line to the Somme, and took over the whole of the Arras sector.

In 1916, the Germans suffered two severe defeats, one before Verdun, and the other on the Somme.

Compelled to remain on the defensive, they fell back on positions prepared beforehand (the Hindenburg Line) from Arras to the north-east of Soissons.

Avoiding the Allies' threatened offensive, they hoped to find greater safety in their new positions, and retard the Allies' further offensives. Scarcely a month after their retreat of March, the Germans were again attacked along an eighteen-mile front, in the Arras sector.

The honour of completely relieving the martyred city of Arras was to fall to the British.

THE BRITISH ATTACKS IN ARTOIS (APRIL-MAY, 1917).
(In liaison with the French Attacks on the Chemin des Dames and Moronvilliers Massif).

The Offensive of April 9.

THE OBJECTIVES. — By their offensive, in liaison with that of the French, on April 16, the British aimed at clearing Arras completely of the enemy, who were still holding Vimy Ridge and the immediate approaches to the town, and by advancing eastwards, they hoped to threaten the important railroad junction of Douai.

METHODS OF ATTACK AND DEFENCE. — Putting to profit the experience gained in the battles of 1916, before Verdun and on the Somme, both sides had improved their methods of attack and defence.

The British had considerably increased the numbers of their guns (all calibres), tanks, scouting and bombing aeroplanes. The methods of attack with limited objective, tried on the Somme (*See* "THE FIRST BATTLE OF THE SOMME"), had been improved, and were now more minutely and more powerfully prepared. Numerous instruction classes had been started, to thoroughly train both officers and men in the new methods of warfare.

Compelled to remain on the defensive, the Germans, determined to prevent a break-through at all cost, had strengthened their positions with new lines of deeply echeloned defences, protected with wire entanglements and blockhouses in reinforced concrete.

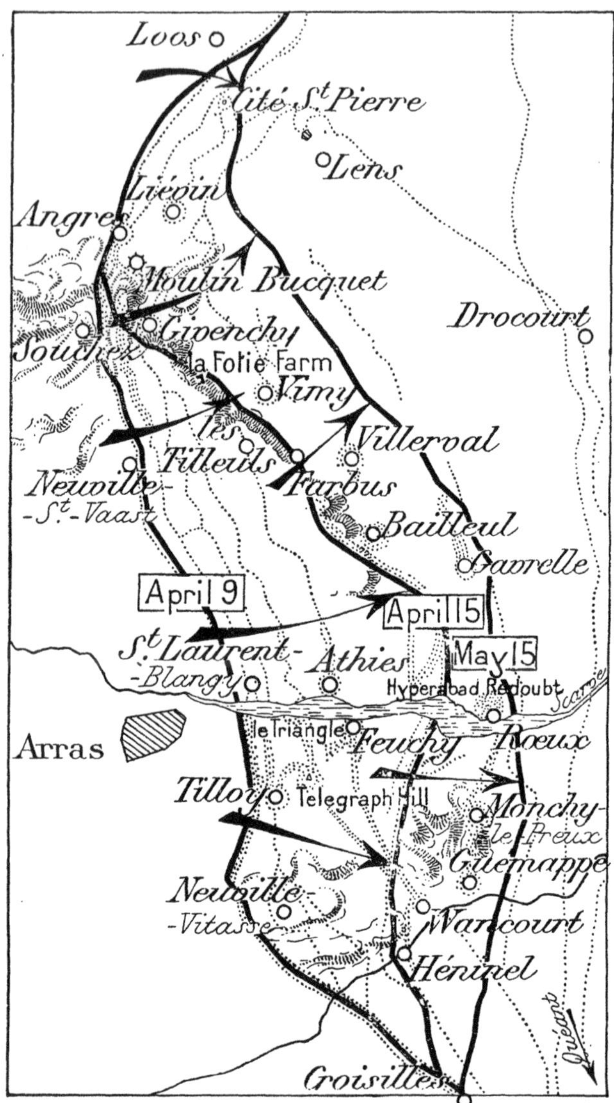

THE BRITISH ATTACKS OF APRIL-MAY 1917, TO RELIEVE ARRAS.

Between Arras and Douai, there existed in 1917, besides the old defences of 1914 and 1915, consisting of three lines of positions, three new positions, one of which was the famous Quéant-Drocourt line, known to the British as "The Switch". The whole formed the newly fortified zone generally referred to as the "Hindenburg Line".

In accordance with Von Below's instructions, the Germans had improved their defensive tactics, by organizing their reserves in view of immediate counter-attacks at given points, where the assailants, after crossing the first positions, were lacking in cohesion.

Preparations for the Attack. — Throughout the winter of 1916 gigantic equipment preparations and a powerful artillery concentration were carried out along the British front of attack, from Lens to Croisilles.

At Arras, in the eastern suburbs, where the opposing trenches touched one another, a veritable underground city was built and comfortably fitted up.

Two British Armies were echeloned between Loos and Croisilles : the 1st Army (Horne), including the famous Canadian Corps, stretched from Loos to Neuville-St-Vaast ; the 3rd Army (Allenby), from Neuville to Croisilles.

In all, there were nineteen divisions in the line, and eleven in reserve, including three cavalry divisions.

The whole of these troops had received a thorough training in mimic attacks against defences similar to those of the enemy.

The Attack. — A violent artillery preparation and a fierce air-battle preceded the attack.

This formidable bombardment, effected in sudden, violent *rafales*, in the various sectors, lasted four days, and crushed the German positions under a deluge of shells of all calibres.

The British airmen flew far behind the German lines, carrying out seventeen bombing raids against the stations, ammunition dumps, mustering-places, etc. In the many air duels, twenty-eight British and fifteen German planes were brought down. Three other enemy machines fell down out of control, and several of their observation-balloons were set on fire. One thousand seven hundred photographs were taken before and during the attack.

The attack was launched on April 9, at 5.30 a. m. The Canadians of the 1st Army dashed to the assault of Vimy Ridge, which had so far proved impregnable, and which for two years the Germans had been fortifying incessantly. In a single rush they carried La Folie Farm and the hamlet of Les Tilleuls ; further south, they captured Hill 132 — marked by the ruins of an old telegraph-station — and the village of Thélus, between Neuville and Farbus.

On the northern spur, the Germans resisted desperately, but were driven back the next day. Violent enemy counter-attacks against the eastern edge of the spur were broken. The Canadians maintained all their positions on the crest, and captured the village and wood of Farbus.

To the east of Arras, the advance on both sides of the Scarpe was still more rapid. The village of St-Laurent-Blangy, which prolongs the eastern suburbs of the town, was carried with fine dash. The British slipped along the Scarpe and the hollows of the neighbouring ground. The second German position, consisting of a strong network of trenches, connecting the villages of Athies and Feuchy, was carried the first day. Tilloy and Neuville-Vitasse were also occupied.

In spite of the inundations from the Scarpe and the destroyed canal, and notwithstanding such formidable positions as the " Triangle ", " Telegraph Hill " and " Hyperabad Redoubt ", the 6th Corps advanced to a depth of five miles.

By April 15, the two British Armies had captured 14,000 prisoners, 19 guns, over a hundred trench mortars, some two hundred machine-guns, and an enormous quantity of war material of all kinds.

The Operations of April-May (*Map p. 16*).

After the brilliant results achieved during the first two days of their offensive, the British consolidated and improved their new positions, by means of local operations. Powerful counter-attacks directed against the eastern edge of Vimy Ridge were repulsed. From April 12 to 15, Angres, Givenchy, Vimy, Villerval and Bailleul were captured.

Whilst, in May, the investment of Lens was begun on the south, by the capture of Bucquet Mill and Liévin, the operations were extended to the north of the town. Starting from Loos, battalions of the 1st Corps carried the St. Pierre suburb, on the north side of the town.

Finally, south of the Scarpe, the British carried the fortified villages of Monchy-le-Preux, Rœux and Guémappe which, since April 10, had successfully resisted all assaults.

Arras was completely cleared of the enemy in May 1917, and the front-line remained fixed on the new positions until March 1918.

THE GERMAN OFFENSIVES OF MARCH 1918.

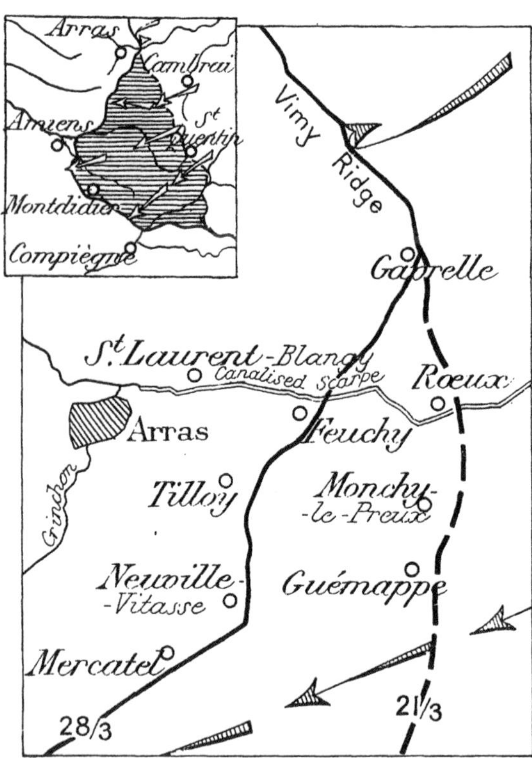

THE GERMAN OFFENSIVE OF MARCH 1918.

North of Arras, it broke down at Vimy Ridge. To the south, the British fell back slightly, in consequence of the retreat on Amiens and Montdidier.

On March 21, Germany, having crushed Russia, began her western campaign of 1918, which she expected would give her the final decision. Putting to profit the experience gained during more than three years of warfare, Ludendorff attacked the British 3rd and 5th Armies along a very wide front, extending from Croisilles to La Fère (50 miles), taking the fullest advantage of the factors of power and surprise: power, by immediately putting into line fifty divisions against the fourteen British divisions; surprise, by carrying out the concentration of all his forces in the greatest secrecy, by a thorough equipment of the whole front, and by a short, violent artillery preparation with gas shells, which overpowered the defenders.

Overwhelmed by numbers, the British wavered and broke, some units fighting to the last man. The battle was carried into the open. Remnants of divisions tried in vain to stay the onrush of the constantly increasing numbers of the enemy. Their French comrades, hurriedly brought up in lorries, threw themselves into the battle, often without waiting for their full equipment. The Allies' resistance, which at first lacked cohesion, was co-ordinated in the thick of the battle. Unity of command was created, and entrusted to Foch.

General Byng.
(*Photo, Russell, London.*)

Thirty-six miles from their base of departure, the German columns passed Montdidier and threatened Amiens, but their thrust eventually died down, and the defenders began to counter-attack. Finally, the enemy onrush spent itself like a wave on the beach (*See* "The Second Battle of the Somme, 1918").

In the Arras sector, the 3rd Army (Byng) resting and pivoting on its left, progressively followed the retreating 5th Army with its right. On March 28, the onrush of the enemy masses at Vimy Ridge and to the south-east of Arras was definitely stayed by the British. North of Arras, the ground conquered in April 1917 was held.

To the south, units of the 3rd Army fell back upon the Feuchy, Tilloy, Neuville-Vitasse line, where they held their ground. The Arras "hinge" withstood all assaults, and the new front-line remained fixed until the end of August 1918.

Drunk with their victories of March-May, the Germans attempted a final assault on the French front in Champagne. This, their "Peace Offensive", failed.

THE ALLIES' LIBERTY OFFENSIVES. July-November 1918.

Grouped under the command of a single chief who knew when and where to strike, and being further very powerfully equipped, the Allied Armies, by a series of carefully timed offensives, forced back the exhausted and demoralized enemy upon their old Hindenburg Line positions.

General Allenby.
(*Photo, F. A. Swaine, London.*)

After the British advance of August 8-12 (*See* "The Second Battle of the Somme 1918") the German lines formed a salient in the Arras sector.

The British decided to attack, in order to turn the German positions on the Somme, and cut off their rail communications to the south-west.

These operations formed the Second Battle of the Scarpe.

The Second Battle of the Scarpe.

In liaison, on the south, with the left wing of Gen. Byng's Army, the Canadians of Gen. Horne's Army attacked on both sides of the Scarpe. The powerful points of support of Rœux and Monchy-le-Preux were carried on August 25. Advancing beyond these centres of resistance, the Canadians followed up their success the next day by capturing Gavrelle and Vis-en-Artois, which brought them into contact with the formidable "Drocourt-Quéant" line. This was broken through on September 2, and the maze of trenches at the junction of this line with the Hindenburg system of defences was carried by storm, the enemy being forced to beat a hasty retreat along the whole front of the Somme.

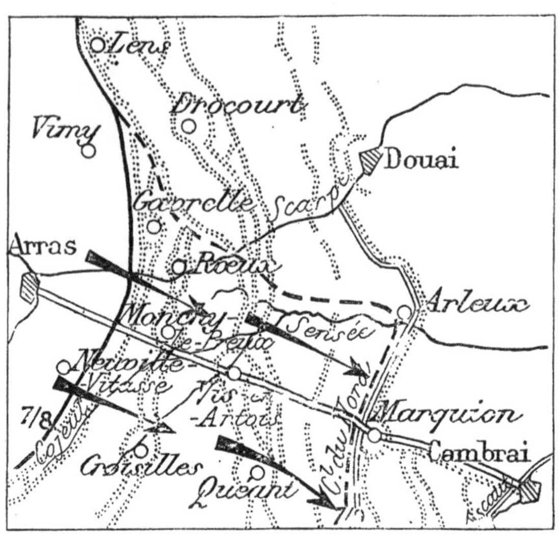

Arras was now definitely cleared. Maintaining their pressure, the Allies next attacked the Hindenburg positions, capturing them one after another. Lens, in ruins, was conquered and passed on October 3. On the 12th, the British were at the gates of Douai.

A month later, the exhausted and demoralized enemy, assailed from all sides, sued for an Armistice.

ARRAS. THE HOTEL-DE-VILLE. (*June 30, 1917*).

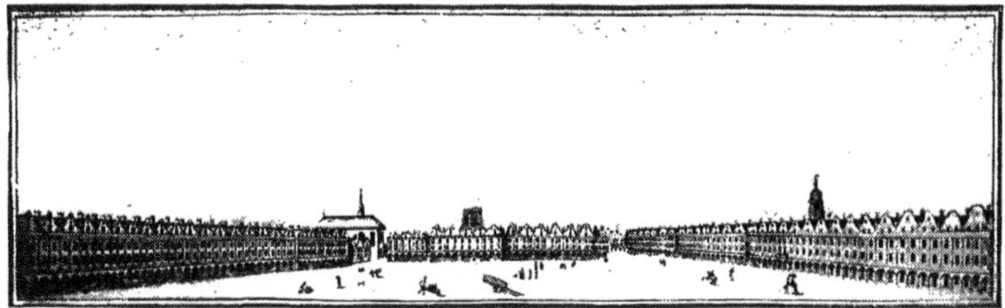

The Grande Place in 1777.

ARRAS.

ORIGIN AND CHIEF HISTORICAL EVENTS.

Of Roman origin, Arras, in the days of Julius Cæsar, was a stronghold defending the roads of invasion of Northern Gaul. The town was built on Baudimont Hill, to the east of the Crinchon, a small stream which runs through Arras. In the 3rd century, it took the name of a tribe which inhabited the district — the *Atrebates* — of which *Arras* is a corruption.

Christianity was preached there during the reign of Clovis, by Saint-Vaast, who created the diocese of Arras and was its first bishop.

In remembrance of the saint, a large abbey, which soon became the most important in the entire region, was erected in the 7th century on the right bank of the Crinchon. Under the protection of this powerful community, a new town gradually grew up around the monastery. Separated at a later date from the original agglomeration by a continuous line of fortifications, the new town was entirely distinct from the old one.

As early as the 11th century, the two places were quite independant of each other, being governed by different authorities, each having its own administration. That built on the site of the ancient Roman city, on Baudimont Hill, to the east, formed the *Cité* of Arras, and was under the bishop's jurisdiction; the other, to the west, constituted the *Ville* proper, and was a dependency of the St. Vaast Abbey. The *Ville* grew steadily, first around the abbey, and later in the neighbourhood of the Hôtel de Ville. The *Cité*, on the contrary, gradually declined until 1749, when it was incorporated in the *Ville*.

Arras was only definitely annexed to the French Realm in 1659, by the Treaty of the Pyrenees. Until then, the *Ville*, as the capital of the County of Artois, successively belonged to the Counts of Flanders (850-1180), to the Counts of Artois (1180-1384), to the Dukes of Burgundy (1384-1492) and finally to the Kings of Spain (1492-1640).

However, the kings of France frequently intervened in the affairs of Arras throughout this period, the *Cité* being always more or less subject to them. On the other hand, the *Ville* only acknowledged the authority of the successive owners of the County of Artois, on whom the Abbey of St. Vaast was dependent. Under the Counts of Flanders, the town was besieged four times by the kings of France in the 9th and 10th centuries. It was granted a Communal Charta by Philippe Auguste in 1194.

THE DESOLATION OF ARRAS DURING THE WAR.
In the foreground: The Hôtel de Ville, Belfry and Petite Place.
In the background: The Grande Place. Wire entanglements cross the squares.

In the 14th century, Arras was torn by popular sedition. Under the Dukes of Burgundy, and especially under Philippe-le-Bon, the town's world-renowned cloth and tapestry industries enjoyed a period of great prosperity. In 1412, Arras is said to have numbered 80,000 inhabitants, i. e. three times its present population. In 1435, Charles VII signed the Treaty of Arras there, with Philippe-le-Bon, by which the Burgundians were released from the English Alliance.

In 1477, at the death of Charles-le-Téméraire, Louis XI claimed the Artois by virtue of the local custom which conferred on him the right to administer the lands of Marie de Bourgogne, heiress to the county. The *Cité* of Arras promptly opened its gates to the Royal Army, but the *Ville* refused to surrender, and was only conquered in 1479, after a long siege. The defenders erected a gibbet on the ramparts, on which they hung the white-crossed banner of France and grotesque figures representing Louis XI, with the inscription: *Veez-ci le roi bochu* (This is the hunchback king). Elsewhere, they wrote this other inscription which long remained famous:

Only when mice catch cats
Will the king be lord of Arras.

A breach was finally made in the ramparts, and Louis XI entered the town. Furious at the people's resistance, he exiled all the inhabitants and peopled the town with newcomers from all parts of France.

The name of Arras was changed to *Franchise*. A few months later, the people of Arras were allowed to return to their homes, and in 1483, on the accession of Charles VIII, the regent, Anne de Beaujeu, restored its ancient name, armorial bearings and laws.

ARRAS. BRITISH MILITARY BAND PLAYING IN THE GRANDE PLACE (*April* 30, 1917).
(*Photo, Imperial War Museum*).

Remembering the treatment inflicted on them by Louis XI, the inhabitants of Arras long remained opposed to French domination. In 1492, they opened their gates to the German and Burgundian troops of Maximilian of Austria, husband of Marie de Bourgogne. However, they lived to regret the change, for as early as that time, the Germans were notorious for their excesses of all kinds. Pillaging was such that the German garrison had to be withdrawn in the following year. *Everything they could lay their hands on*, wrote a contemporary chronicler, *was rifled and held to ransom, the immense quantities of utensils, crockery, jewelry and chains were such that their coffers could not hold them.* (JEAN MOLINET'S Chronicles).

Meanwhile, the Spanish remained masters of Arras, which only again came under the rule of the kings of France in 1640, when it fell after a long and bloody siege. The bombardments caused great damage. According to the diary of one, Gérard Robert, projectiles were daily hurled from the *Cité* into Arras, by "mortars" posted in different places. St. Vaast and its enclosure suffered especially. The vaulting of the nave of the church was pierced, the great damage being promptly repaired by order of the king. Fourteen missiles, some of them measuring fifty-two "*paule*" in circumference, fell on the dormitory and in other places.

Fourteen years later (1654), the Prince de Condé with a Spanish army 45,000 strong, invested Arras.

The town held out heroically, and was delivered after a forty-five day siege by a relief force commanded by Turenne (August 25, 1654).

Arras lived through troublous times during the Revolution. In

1793, the Conventioner, Joseph Le Bon, sent there on a mission, organized the Terror. The guillotine was permanently erected in the Place de la Comédie. *The Terror was such that travellers would go ten leagues out of their way to avoid passing through Arras. If one were in the street, it was a conspiracy, a plot. The merchants ceased their business, and out of fear, attended the sittings of the Tribunal and Popular Society.* (Trial of Joseph Le Bon).

During the Franco-German War (1870-71), the Germans got as far as the gates of Arras, but did not enter the city.

The following persons were born at Arras : Adam de la Halle, bard, and the pitiless conventioners Maximilian and Augustin Robespierre and Joseph Le Bon, who were guillotined at the fall of the Terror.

The Boves — A local Curiosity.

A large number of houses in Arras possess several stories of superimposed cellars of very ancient origin, called " Boves ", which were formerly quarries of soft stone.

Formerly, the first floor of the sub-basement was often fitted up as a tavern, dwelling, or workshop.

Stone columns with capitals, sometimes 12th or 13th century, support the vaulting, which is either semicircular or groined.

Many of these cellars still have chimneys, stoves, etc.

Below this first sub-basement, one and sometimes two more storeys of " boves " were hollowed out of the limestone rock. These cellars have neither vaulting nor decoration, but in some of them are pits, from which the stone, used in the construction of the town, was extracted.

" Boves " are to be found practically everywhere in Arras, except in the low-lying quarters, where the Crinchon stream runs underground. The most remarkable are those which were made under the Grande Place (12th century), under the old Hôtel des Rosettes and under the Place de la Préfecture.

13th CENTURY HOUSE IN THE GRANDE PLACE (No. 49).
The Gable and Roof are 16th Century.
On the ground-floor is seen the entrance to the cellars or " boves ".

Since very early times, the " boves " have ranked among the chief curiosities of Arras.

In his description of the Low-Countries, Guichardin wrote several centuries ago :

In all the houses there are finely vaulted caves and cellars. These were purposely built wide and deep, so that in time of war whole families might find shelter there from the fury of the enemy's cannon.

In the last century, another writer gave the following description : *In Arras, most of the cellars are inhabited. The doors are always open, to the great risk of the passers-by, who fall in, if they pass too near the houses. The interiors are hideous, as there is no light but that which comes in through the door, and no air. There is only one miserable bed for the whole family.*

These underground cellars were used during the Great War. As in the bygone days of Guichardin, the inhabitants of Arras found in them a shelter " from the fury of the enemy's cannon ".

Arras during the Great War.

The Germans occupied Arras only three days, entering the town on September 6, 1914 and being forced to withdraw on the 9th.

The usual looting excepted, they did not commit any special acts of violence, but levied heavy requisitions both in money and kind.

Almost immediately after their departure, the " Martyrdom of Arras " began. The Germans remained at the very gates of the city, investing the latter from north to south at a very short distance from it. In places, they were scarcely four kilometres away. The cemetery situated in the suburb of St. Sauveur (behind the station) had to be organized defensively. Deep trenches intersected it in all directions (*photo below*).

TRENCHES IN THE CEMETERY.

The siege lasted until April 1917, i.e. 31 months.

The innumerable bombardments began on October 6, 1914. On the 6th, 7th, and 8th of that month, over 1,000 shells fell in the town, the station and barracks of which only were occupied militarily. The gunners fired ceaselessly on the central quarters, the two famous squares, forming the finest monumental decoration of the town, being their principal targets.

On October 7, the HOTEL DE VILLE was burnt down, whilst a few days later, the BELFRY was brought down by 69 shells.

Afterwards, the bombardments slackened, yet every day, bombs reminded the inhabitants that the enemy were at the city gates. At times, the artillery fire would break out again, with great fury. For instance, on July 9, 1915, nearly 6,000 shells, most of them incendiary, burst in Arras, completing its ruin, and setting fire to the old ABBEY OF ST. VAAST and to the CATHEDRAL.

Other equally violent bombardments took place in 1916 and in the first months of 1917. Until the offensive of April 1917, which cleared the town, Arras never experienced an hour's respite.

At that time, 962 buildings had been completely destroyed, 1,595 damaged beyond repair, and 1,735 badly hit, but capable of restoration.

Out of the 4,521 houses forming the town (exclusive of the suburbs), only 292 escaped injury.

The martyrdom of Arras was not yet, however, complete. In March 1918, when the great German Offensive began, the bombardments broke out afresh, causing new ruins and bringing down those buildings which had until then escaped destruction. The last of the inhabitants, those who, in spite of all, had continued to cling to their homes, had to be evacuated. Five months later, at the end of August 1918, the British broke through the German lines before Arras, and drove the enemy for good out of artillery range of the unfortunate city.

AFTER THE VICTORY.

The return of the 33rd Regiment of the line to Arras, in April 1919.

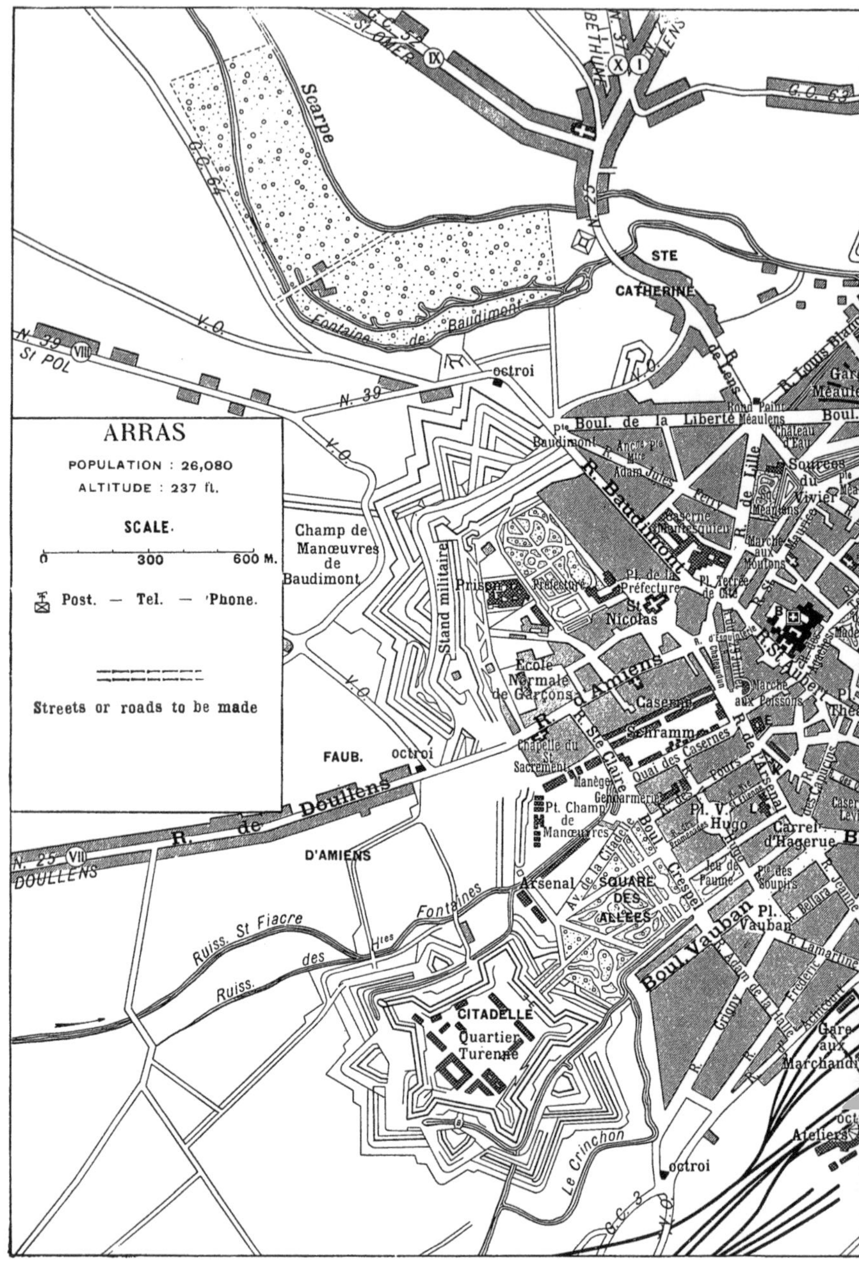
ARRAS
POPULATION : 26,080
ALTITUDE : 237 ft.
SCALE.
0
300
600 M.
Post. — Tel. — 'Phone.
Streets or roads to be made
Scarpe
Fontaine de Baudimont
STE
CATHERINE
octroi
Champ de Manœuvres de Baudimont
Stand militaire
Prison
Préfecture
St Nicolas
École Normale de Garçons
R. Baudimont
Boul. de la Liberté
FAUB.
D'AMIENS
R. de Doullens
CITADELLE
Quartier Turenne
Arsenal
SQUARE DES ALLÉES
Boul. Vauban
Pl. Vauban
Ruiss. St Fiacre
Le Crinchon
Gare aux Marchandis
Ateliers

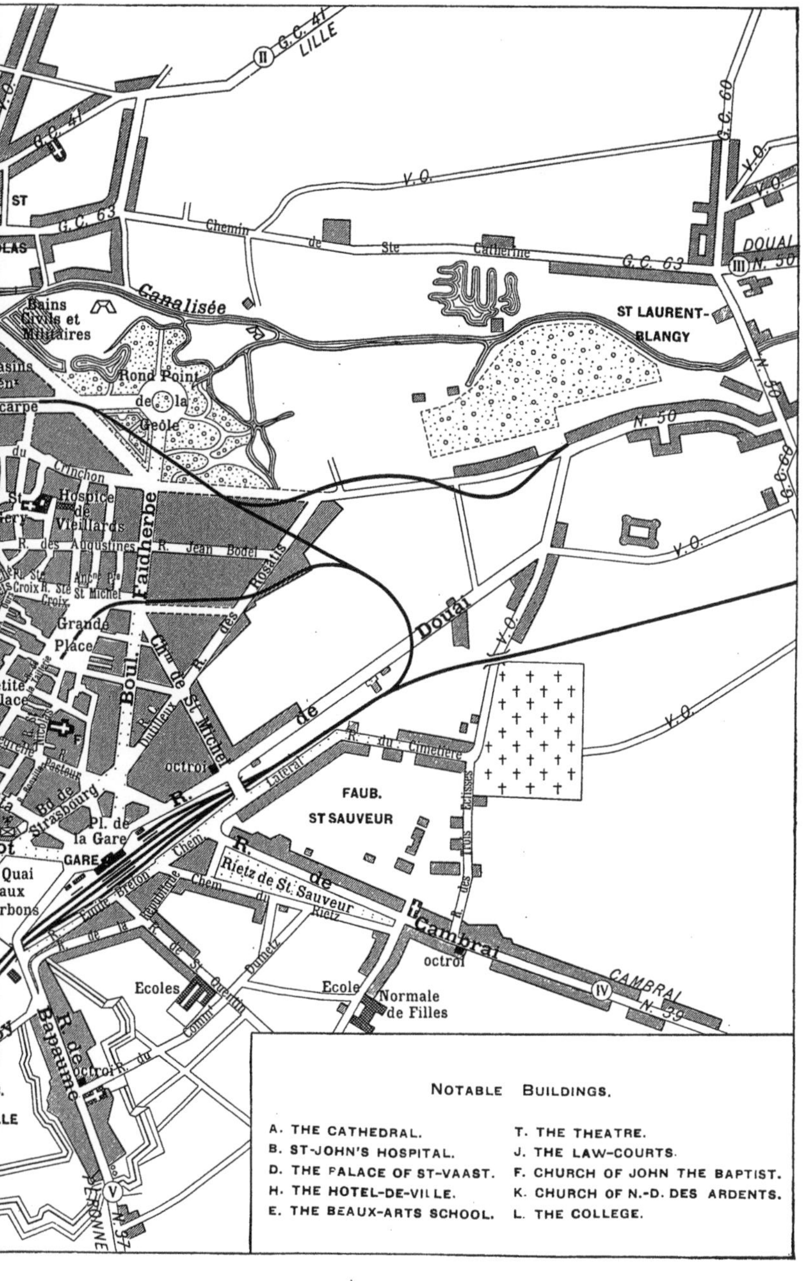
G.C. 41
LILLE
G.C. 41
G.C. 63
ST
Chemin de Ste Catherine
V.O.
G.C. 60
G.C. 63
DOUAI
N. 50
Canalisée
Bains Civils et Militaires
Rond Point de la Geôle
ST LAURENT-BLANGY
N. 50
G.C. 60
du Crinchon
Hospice de Vieillards
R. des Augustines
R. Jean Bodel
Faidherbe
R. des Rosatis
Grande Place
Petite Place
Boul.
Chin de St Michel
R. de Douai
octroi
FAUB. ST SAUVEUR
R. du Cimetière
Latéral
R. des trois Eclisses
Bd de Strasbourg
Pl. de la Gare
GARE
Quai aux Charbons
R. Emile Breton
Chem.
Rietz de St. Sauveur
Chem. du Rietz
R. de Cambrai
octroi
CAMBRAI
N. 39
R. de St Quentin
R. Dumetz
Ecoles
Ecole Normale de Filles
R. de Bapaume
octroi
PERONNE
N. 37
NOTABLE BUILDINGS.
A. THE CATHEDRAL.
B. ST-JOHN'S HOSPITAL.
D. THE PALACE OF ST-VAAST.
H. THE HOTEL-DE-VILLE.
E. THE BEAUX-ARTS SCHOOL.
T. THE THEATRE.
J. THE LAW-COURTS.
F. CHURCH OF JOHN THE BAPTIST.
K. CHURCH OF N.-D. DES ARDENTS.
L. THE COLLEGE.

A VISIT TO ARRAS.

From the Station to the Petite Place (*See plan below*).

Start from the Place de la Gare.

The Station, a large stone and brick building, was erected in 1898 on the site of the old fortifications. At the end of the war, it was in ruins and had to be almost entirely rebuilt.

Take the Rue Gambetta, opposite the station.

This street forms the beginning of the great artery which crossed the town from end-to-end, from the south-east to the north-west, under the names of the Rue Gambetta, the Rue Ernestale, the Rue St. Aubert and the Rue Baudimont.

The quarters of the old *Ville*, to the north, should be visited first.

To the south, lie those of the lower town, and of the ancient *Cité* (*See p.* 32).

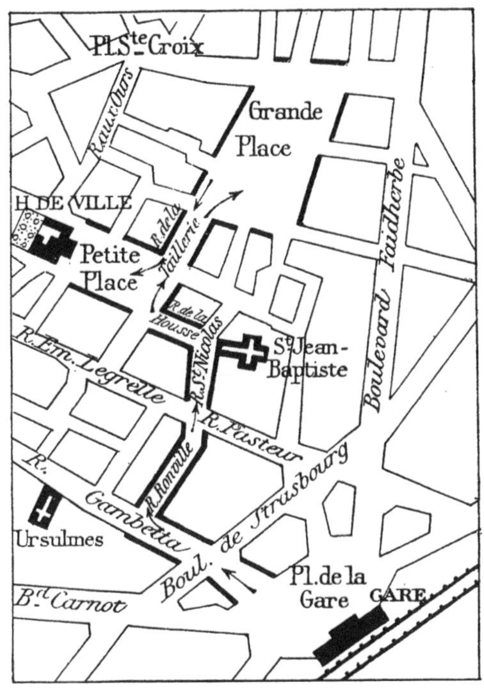

Follow the roads shown by thick lines.

The Place de la Gare.

In the middle: The Rue Gambetta, in which the General Post Office *and the ruined tower of the* Chapelle des Ursulines *may be distinguished.*

CHAPELLE DES URSULINES, *before the War.* (*Cliché LL.*)

Follow the Rue Gambetta and cross the Boulevard de Strasbourg. At the corner, on the left, is the GENERAL POST-OFFICE, which was damaged by the shells (*Photo p.* 27).

Further on, to the left, is the curious tower of the CHAPELLE DES URSULINES (1862), an enlarged copy of the ancient CHAPELLE DE LA SAINTE-CHANDELLE which, until 1791, stood in the Petite Place (*See p.* 33). The tower consists of a square base surmounted by another square portion placed cornerwise on the first.

A third octogonal story with a spire completed the building. The bombardments destroyed this story, which had previously lost its spire in 1876, during a storm (*Photos*).

Turn to the right (100 *yards before the Chapelle des Ursulines*) *into the Rue Ronville, then take the Rue St. Nicolas, which prolongs it. On the right, is* the mutilated façade of the CHURCH OF JOHN-THE-BAPTIST (*Photos p.* 29).

This, the most ancient church in Arras, was destroyed by the shells.

The vaulting and upper portions of the pillars and walls have fallen down. Built in 1565-1584 in the Gothic style, it comprised three naves and a choir terminating in a hemi-cycle.

A high, massive stone tower was added in the 18th century.

Under the Revolution, the Church of John-the-Baptist became a Temple of Reason.

A miniature mountain of masonry was built in the interior, at the top of which was placed a Statue of Liberty.

CHAPELLE DES URSULINES IN 1920.

Soon afterwards (Messidor 23, Year III of the Republic), the Municipality had this "mountain" replaced by a pedestal, and ordered the red bonnets of the personages of the pictures in the temple to be painted tricolour.

The church of John-the-Baptist contained some fine wood-work and two famous pictures: *The Descent from the Cross*, attributed to Rubens, and *The Assumption*, attributed to Philippe de Champaigne.

These works have been saved.

Opposite the church, take the Rue de la Housse, leading to the Petite Place.

Turn to the right, then keep straight on, via the Rue de la Taillerie (Photo p. 30) to the GRANDE PLACE, *which visit.* (*See p.* 31).

RUE ST-NICOLAS
AND CHURCH OF JOHN-THE-BAPTIST, IN 1914. (*Cliché LL*).

Return to the PETITE PLACE, *by the same way* (*See p.* 33).

THE FAÇADE OF JOHN-THE-BAPTIST CHURCH IN 1919.

The Squares of Arras.

The GRANDE and PETITE PLACE of Arras formed an architectural *ensemble* unique in France. For centuries, private houses all having the same general arrangement, had bordered these squares. Monolithic columns of stone, adorned with Doric capitals, and linked up by elliptical arches, supported the vaulted gallery which ran round each of the two squares, and on which opened the entrances to the houses. The latter, which touched one another, were ornamented, above their two brick-and-stone stories, with irregular, voluted gables of varied outline, pierced with round or oval windows.

The gables, further adorned with scroll-work, terminated in circular pediments.

The Rue de la Taillerie (*Photo below*), which connected the two squares, was bordered with houses in the same style. In all, there were three hundred and forty-five stone columns and one hundred and fifty-five arcaded and gabled houses.

These houses dated from the 12th and 13th centuries, the original constructions being of wood. Massive beams supported the galleries and the wooden façades of the houses. The two squares were then known as the " Grand Marché " and " Petit Marché ". The porticos gave shelter to the shop-keepers' stalls, the varied merchandise of which drew motley crowds of buyers.

The basements at the back of the galleries, and lighted by the latter, served as dwellings, shops and factories. It was in these damp cellars that the stuffs and tapestries of Arras, so highly reputed in the Middle-Ages, were made.

The bombardments of 1640 and 1654 demolished or severely damaged a large number of the houses. The façades were rebuilt in stone, not as is commonly believed in the Spanish, but in the Flemish style.

Both the squares are now in ruins.

THE RUE DE LA TAILLERIE.

Connecting up the GRANDE *and the* PETITE PLACE. *The latter is seen in the photo.*

THE GRANDE PLACE BEFORE THE WAR.
In the background: THE BELFRY.

The Grande Place.

Seventy-five façades used to adorn the Grande Place, which was formerly an orchard belonging to the Abbey of St. Vaast. The side facing east, has been almost entirely destroyed. The three other sides were less damaged.

Almost all these houses dated from the 17th century, and long retained their picturesque names: *Le Chapeau Amoureux*, *La Grande Autruche*, *Le Vieil Tripot*, *L'Ange*, *L'Epée Royale*, *Le Griffon Volant*, *La Grosse Tête*, *La Madeleine*, *La Fleur de Lys*, *la Brique d'Or*, etc.

THE GRANDE PLACE IN 1919. (*See above*).
THE BELFRY *has disappeared.*

RUINS OF AN ANCIENT HOUSE IN THE GRANDE PLACE.

Many had old and curious signs carved in the stone-work, among others: *Les Rosettes* (No. 17), *Le Chapeau Vert* (No. 59), *La Cloche* (No. 72), *Le Mouton d'Argent* (No. 56), *Le Heaume* (No. 46, 14th century), *Le Chaudron* (No. 32), *Les Bons Amis* (No. 8).

The latter, dating from 1635, represented two men shaking hands near a forge.

Several houses were earlier than the 17th century. The oldest — No. 49 — with a double gable having a 16th century turret, dated back to the 13th century. It escaped uninjured (*Photo p.* 24.)

Most of the houses were built over several superimposed cellars or "boves" dating from the Middle-Ages (*See p.* 24). The most interesting "boves" are those underneath the ancient *hôtels "des Rosettes"* (No. 17) (12th century) and "*du Heaume*" (No. 46). These two houses were formerly famous hostelries. In the 15th century, the knights who were invited by the Dukes of Burgundy to take part in the tournaments and jousting in the Grande Place, used to stay there.

The Grande Place was both a place of public amusement and an important market for corn and cattle, being in the 19th century the most important in the whole region. The entire population of Arras and the outlying districts used to meet there on Saturdays and fair-days. The market extended as far as the Petite Place, when both squares would be covered with a multitude of white or green tents, in which were the stalls of the merchants. Here the people of the town and neighbouring villages would throng together, bargaining, exchanging news and discussing local politics. The animation reached its highest pitch in the drinking booths.

"*Here the people met together to seal bargains, strengthen old friendships and ruin their stomachs with corrosive liquors* ("*bistouilles*") *or Arras beer.*" (C. ENLART's "Arras avant la Guerre"). Then, when all was quiet, pigeons would settle in thousands on the ground and pick up the scattered grain.

The Petite Place.

The houses in the Rue de la Taillerie, which connects the Grande with the Petite Place, have suffered less. There is a fine Renaissance façade in the yard of No. 15.

The Petite Place was bordered, on the west, by the HOTEL DE VILLE above which rose the graceful silhouette of the BELFRY. On the other three sides were 52 arcaded and gabled houses, 21 of which were completely destroyed.

The Petite Place was long the centre of the town. The people used to gather there, in front of the Hôtel de Ville, for public meetings, festivals, and also for public executions.

The undermentioned buildings, destroyed in the 18th century or during the Revolution, formerly stood in the square.

To the east, opposite the Hôtel de Ville, a massive fortress with turrets, erected in the reign of Philippe-le-Bon, Duke of Burgundy, and known as the "Maison Rouge", either because it was built of brick, or on account of the executions which took place in front of it. It was first designed as a check on the bellicose tendencies of the citizens of Arras, being later used as a "Bourse" or banking-house. It was pulled down in 1757.

In the centre, stood the Chapelle du Saint-Cierge, in which the "Holy Candle" of Arras was kept (*see p.* 56). Erected in the Petite Place, at the beginning of the 13th century, by the Brotherhood of Notre-Dame-des-Ardents, it was rebuilt several times in the course of the succeeding centuries, and notably after the bombardments of 1640. It was surmounted by a Gothic tower, the primitive arrangement of which was reproduced in the spire of the Chapelle des Ursulines (*see p.* 28).

THE PETITE PLACE IN 1773. (*Drawing by J. V. David*).
In the centre : THE CHAPELLE DU ST-CIERGE, *where the* "HOLY CANDLE" *was kept* (*see p.* 56).

THE RUE DES BALANCES. GENERAL VIEW OF THE RUINS OF THE

Near the entrance to the Rue St. Géry, stood a stone cross with an iron collar, to which criminals were attached.

THE RUINS OF THE HOTEL DE VILLE AND BELFRY.
The Rue Vinocq. — On the right, in the background : THE PETITE PLACE.

As in the Grande Place, each house in the Petite Place had its own name, in the 17th century.

Among others were : *La Rose, Le Soleil d'Or, L'Asne Rayé, L'Espingle d'Argent, La Grappe d'Or, Les Louchettes, Le Pastoureau, Le Haubert, Le Dragon,* etc.

Numerous carved signs had kept alive these old names, the most curious being : *Le Limaçon* (No. 7, late 15th century), *Le Bar d'Or* (No. 8), *Les Trois Coqs* or *Coquelets* (No. 9), *La Sirène* (No. 11), whose escutcheon represented the sea, with ships, and a mermaid looking in a hand mirror), *L'Amiral* (No. 15) representing a man, telescope in hand, looking at the sea, and a vessel tossed by the waves, *La Licorne d'Or* (No. 23), *La Harpe* (No. 42) depicting a harp

PETITE PLACE, HOTEL DE VILLE, AND BELFRY. THE RUE DE LA TAILLERIE.

entwined with leaves and fruit, *Le Peigne d'Or* (No. 52), *La Baleine* (No. 64), etc.

The ruins of the Hôtel de Ville are on the west side of the Petite Place, on which the oldest and most beautiful façade stood.

Take the Rue de la Braderie, which, after skirting the right wing of the building (*Photo*, p. 39), *leads to the Place de la Vacquerie.*

The rear façade of the Hôtel de Ville overlooked this square (*Photo* p. 40).

THE PETITE PLACE, BEFORE THE WAR. (*Cliché LL.*).

The Town-Hall and Belfry.

Although, throughout the Middle-Ages, Arras was a powerful *commune*, invested with administrative, legislative and legal powers, it had no *Maison Commune* or Hôtel de Ville until the end of the 16th century.

Until that time, the municipal magistrates, mayor and sheriffs met together in a small room in the Rue St. Géry, to draw up the ordinances relating to the local militia, taxes, etc., and to administer justice. The *bancloque*, i. e. the bell used for proclamations and to call together the burghers or representatives of the *commune*, was installed in the tower of the Church of St. Géry.

In 1463, the sheriffs decided to erect a belfry in the Petite Place, as a symbol of their communal liberties. The work was interrupted during the agitations which prevailed in Arras towards the end of the 15th century, and it was only in 1499 that the tower was completed, in accordance with the original plans. Later (1551) the Belfry was raised and crowned in the style of the Flemish belfry of Audenaerde. Meanwhile, by virtue of a decision of the town's burghers in 1501, a fine Hôtel de Ville, overlooking the Petite Place, had been built in front of the Belfry, to replace the Sheriffs' Hall in the Rue St. Géry, which was then falling into ruin.

The Hôtel de Ville (1501-1517), Gothic-Flamboyant in style, presented the same general arrangement as that of St. Quentin, the façade of which was completed in 1509.

The ground-floor formed an ogive-vaulted gallery opening on the Petite Place, with seven arcades of unequal width supported by octagonal columns of stone. Between the arcades, surmounted with archivolts and ornamented with finely carved foliage, a number of small niches with brackets and sculptured canopies were hollowed out.

The high façade of the first story, which terminated by a balustrade with flamboyant ornamentation, was pierced with eight drop-arched mullioned windows, with niches in between. Above the windows, between the ends of the crowning arches, which were also richly ornamented with fine foliate carving, opened seven round windows.

Lastly, came the high steep roof pierced with three rows of small dormer-windows with lead ornamentation and gilded weathercocks.

In the 16th century, a small covered platform or "bretèche" was built in the middle of the first story, from which the magistrates took the oath, addressed the people, and caused the municipal by-laws to be read out. The platform was removed in the 18th century, and replaced by an eighth window with a balustraded balcony.

On each side of the façade was a Renaissance pavilion, set somewhat back. That on the right was modern, whilst the left-hand one dated from 1572.

The main building was 16th century and comprised a ground-floor and two stories lighted by windows with stone mullions. The windows were separated by twin columns, the style differing with each storey. Above this richly decorated entablature, three highly ornamented dormer-windows opened out at the base of the roof. A curious exterior staircase, surmounted with a small cupola, gave access in the 16th century to the pavilion. It was pulled down in the 18th century.

THE HOTEL DE VILLE AND BELFRY BEFORE THE WAR.
The Façade in the Petite Place. *Compare with photo, p. 38.*

The Hôtel-de-Ville was considerably enlarged under the Second Empire, by the addition of a wing in the Rue de la Braderie and the over decorated Renaissance rear façade overlooking the Place de la Vacquerie.

The Hôtel de Ville was destroyed by the German guns early in October 1914. The façade in the Petite Place, including the Renaissance Pavilion, no longer exists. The other three façades were reduced to shapeless ruins with, here and there, fragments of architecture and ornamentation.

The Belfry, seen from the Petite Place. (*Compare with photo, p. 37*).

The Belfry.

Abutting on the rear façade of the *Maison Commune*, there was a lofty graceful Belfry, — the pride of Arras.

It was destroyed a few days after the Hôtel de Ville.

THE RUINS OF THE HOTEL-DE-VILLE.
The corner of the Rue de la Braderie and the Place de la Vacquerie. In the background:
THE PETITE PLACE.

On October 21, 1914, after being struck by 69 shells, it collapsed. Only the stone basement remains, surrounded by débris.

The Belfry of Arras was the highest in France. A staircase of 365 steps led to the top. It was inaugurated in 1554.

An ancient inscription in the Watch Tower reads:

L'an mil cincq cens cinquante quatre
Par un second jour de juillet,
Jehan Delamotte et Pierre Goulattre
Firent en ce lieu le premier ghuet.

(*In the year* 1554, *on the second day of July, Jehan Delamotte and Pierre Goulattre kept their first watch here.*).

From that time forward, a bell was rung, each morning and evening at the opening and closing of the city gates. Immediately afterwards, a bugler and three hautboy-players, paid by the town, played an air of music.

The watchmen rang the bell not only to announce sunrise and curfew, but also to warn the people when danger threatened the town, to call the burghers to the assemblies, and on the occasion of all important events, e.g. triumphal entries into Arras, festivals, public rejoicings, etc...

For these different occasions, Arras possessed a whole series of bells:

The " Alarme ", " Effroy ", or " Sang " bell, dating from 1433, and cast in bronze. Flat shaped, it was hung in the stone crown of the belfry.

The " Retraite " or " Couvre-feu " bell, dating from 1483.

The " Guet " or " Répétition " bell, dating from 1682, and lastly

THE HOTEL DE VILLE AND BELFRY IN 1920.
The Façade in the Place de la Vacquerie. On the right : The Rue Vinocq ; On the left : The Rue de la Braderie. *Compare with photo, p. 41.*

the " Ban " or " Bancloque " bell weighing about nine tons. It was cracked in 1464, during the festivals held in honour of Louis XI's stay in Arras. It was re-cast a first time, then again in 1728, when it was christened " Joyeuse ", being used principally on days of public rejoicing. Not to endanger the tower, the bell had not been rung for many years prior to the War.

Fragments of the bells were found buried under the ruins of the Hôtel de Ville.

The Belfry was twice rebuilt. To the square base begun in 1463 and completed towards the end of the 15th century, were added three octagonal stories in 1551. The entire edifice was in the Gothic style.

The square base was supported at each corner by two buttresses terminating in crocketed pinnacles. On each front opened two drop-arched bays over a double row of blind arcading.

About 150 feet from the ground, an open-work gallery ran round this square tower concealing the octagonal base of the upper stories erected in 1551-1554 by the master-mason Jacques Le Caron de Marchiennes. A native of Vaux-lès-Bapaume, he is described in a commemorative tablet, put up at the time the tower was completed, as a master in this art, and of great renown.

The first story of the upper portion of the belfry was stayed by small flying-buttresses supported by piers, surmounted with sculptured pinnacles. On each side was a dial of the clock, which was thus visible from every quarter of the town.

Above a second open-work gallery, rose the narrower second story

THE HÔTEL DE VILLE AND BELFRY. THE FAÇADE IN THE PLACE DE LA VACQUERIE.
Compare with photo, page 40.

surrounded by eight piers with flying buttresses, behind which opened eight small bays provided with sound-reflectors. The bell-chamber, containing a peal of 24 small bells, was installed here. The third and still narrower story was supported by another open-work gallery. Inside, was the small room in which the city watchmen used to keep watch. A ducal crown formed the roof of this room, being itself surmounted by a heraldic lion of bronze which, 244 feet above the ground, held the unfolded banner of Arras.

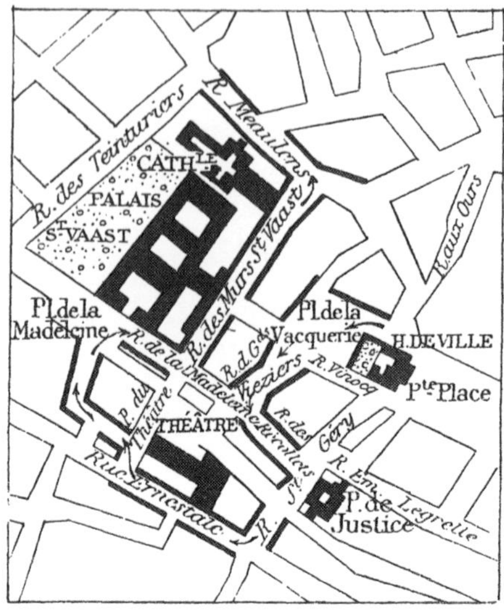

Follow the roads shown by thick lines.

From the Petite Place to the Cathedral.

Continue to visit the town, leaving the Place de la Vacquerie, behind the Hôtel de Ville.

The houses in the Square were very severely damaged by the bombardments, especially on the south side, where many of them were completely razed. Skirt this devasted area, following the Rue des Grands-Viéziers and then the Rue des Récollets, which branches off to the left.

The latter street leads to the Rue St. Géry, which take to the right. Before turning notice one of the façades of the Palais de Justice (*photo below*), situated on the right of the Rue Legrelle, which prolongs the Rue des Récollets. The main building faces the Rue St. Géry, which the tourist now takes. The Palais de Justice escaped practically undamaged.

Erected in 1724, on the site of the house which, until the completion of the Hôtel de Ville, was used as the Sheriff's Hall by the burghers of Arras, this fine building was formerly the ancient "hôtel" of the States of Artois.

Underneath the Palais de Justice is a large 13th century cellar,

THE PALAIS DE JUSTICE. THE FAÇADE IN THE RUE LEGRELLE.

measuring 55 feet by 24 feet, with ogival vaulting resting on stone columns.

Keep along the Rue St. Géry, which ends at the point where the Rue Ernestale prolongs the Rue Gambetta.

Turn to the right into the Rue Ernestale, which leads to the Petite PLACE DU THÉATRE, *on the right.*

It was in this square, then called the Place de la Comédie, that the guillotine was installed, during the Terror. From one of the theatre balconies, the Pro-Consul Joseph Le Bon and his wife applauded the executions, in number more than five hundred.

The theatre, dating from the end of the 18th century, was of no particular interest.

MAISON DES POISSONNIERS, *in the Place du Théâtre.*

In the square, the MAISON DES POISSONNIERS, which escaped damage, has a curious 17th century façade, greatly disfigured, however, by later restorations. Built in the same style as the façades in the Petite and Grande Places, the ancient covered gallery

THE PALAIS ST. VAAST.
The Principal Entrance in the Place de la Madeleine.

The Palais St. Vaast and the Cathedral, before the War.

on the ground-floor was replaced by a shop. It is decorated with carvings representing a Triton and two mermaids. On the gable, rebuilt in the 19th century and terminating in a circular pediment, two other mermaids, arranged as consoles, on either side of the window, replaced two seated statues symbolising the rivers Crinchon and Scarpe.

The Rue des Rapporteurs (at No. 5 in which Robespierre was born), opposite the theatre, leads to the Place de la Madeleine.

The Palais St.-Vaast has its main entrance in this square.

The Ancient Abbey or Palais St. Vaast.

The old Abbey of St. Vaast was founded in 687 by Bishop St. Aubert in commemoration of St. Vaast, who was the first to preach Christianity in Arras.

Thanks to the favour and liberality of King Thierry III, it prospered rapidly. Destroyed by the Normans in the 9th century, it was later burnt down on three different occasions, only to rise again from its ruins. Under Spanish rule, it became the most important religious community in the Low Countries.

In the Middle Ages, the Monastery, then under Benedictine rule, comprised an agglomeration of buildings, which grew in proportion as the Abbey's prosperity increased. However, with the exception of its Gothic Church, the Monastery was of no special architectural interest.

The place fell into ruin and was demolished in 1746. Rebuilding was begun in 1754, but the new Abbey was scarcely completed (1784) when the Revolution broke out, and the building was taken over for lay purposes.

The Palais St. Vaast is about 720 feet long and 260 feet wide.

THE PALAIS ST. VAAST AND THE CATHEDRAL IN 1919.

In the 19th century, the Bishop's apartments, the Grand Seminary of Arras, the Museum, the Municipal Library and the Offices of the County Archives were all housed in its vast premises.

During the War it was wilfully and methodically burnt by the Germans. Although the old monastery served no military purpose, the Germans bombarded it with great violence on July 6, 1915, the incendiary shells setting fire to the Museum, Library and Archives. Whilst the Palace was burning, the Germans encircled it with a barrage of artillery fire, making all attempts to fight the flames futile.

Today, nothing remains but the charred walls of the outer and inner façades, which were of such massive construction as to resist the action both of the shells and fire.

The Abbey was built in the stiff academic style of the 18th century.

The main entrance, decorated with statues of Religion and Science, is in the Place de la Madeleine (*Photo, p.* 43). Through it is reached the Court of Honour, surrounded with two-storied buildings arranged in a semi-circle.

Behind the Court of Honour are two other courts surrounded by buildings more or less in ruins. The first is square in shape, the second rectangular, and bordered with vaulted cloisters of fine proportions. These were formerly the Great and Small Cloisters of the Abbey, and now bear numerous traces of the bombardments.

At the end of the Great Cloister, a vaulted peristyle of imposing appearance, supported by two rows of Ionic columns (*photo, p.* 48), leads to the south transept of the old Abbey church, which, in the 19th century, became the Cathedral of Arras. This church was also ruined by fire and shells.

Inside the old Abbey were to be seen: the monks' refectory, with

THE MUSEUM DURING THE WAR.
The works of art were removed to the cellars, the latter being protected and consolidated.

its six high windows, finely carved wood panelling, and a great red marble fireplace over seven feet high and nearly fifteen feet wide; the library, a spacious hall about 160 feet long and two stories high; fine ceilings, staircases and ornamental wrought-iron and woodwork.

Underneath the buildings are roomy cellars with groined vaulting. It was here that the art treasures of Arras were stored during the War (*photo above*). The left (west) wing of the Palais St. Vaast contained the county archives, library and museum, before the War.

The archives were both numerous and valuable, and included a very complete collection of charters, known as the *Trésor des Chartes d'Artois* (13th and 14th centuries), also numerous documents from the Abbey of St. Vaast (Védastine), and from other ancient and important abbeys in the district.

The library contained about 40,000 volumes and 1,100 MSS. Some illuminated MSS, both liturgical and secular, dating from various periods, were of especial interest, as were also numerous genealogical collections belonging to the 18th century.

The archives and library were partly destroyed by fire in July 1915. However, most of the MSS and the more valuable books and documents were removed to a place of safety, either before the fire, or while the Palais was still burning.

The Museum.

The collections of the Museum, which included an interesting archæological section and numerous picture galleries, suffered considerable damage, but the principal works of art were saved.

The archæological gallery included the following noteworthy collections: Series of antiques, especially some Merovingian jewels, the

TOMBSTONE OF GUILLAUME-LE-FRANÇOIS (*15th Century*).

tomb of Bishop Frumaud, decorated with mosaic (1183); several other carved tombstones, especially that of Guillaume-le-François (15th century), on which is the figure of a decomposed body of striking realism (*photo above*); a fine 14th century marble head of a woman (*photo below*); numerous fragments of architecture and sculpture, taken from the ancient cathedral of Arras, and including some fine 12th or 13th century capitals.

Part ot the galleries of the lapidary museum were buried under a heap of rubbish several yards deep, caused by the bombardments. Many ancient pieces of sculpture were recovered practically intact, when the débris were cleared away.

The picture galleries contained some valuable paintings, belonging mostly to the 16th century (Flemish School), 17th century, and modern schools.

The Museum further contained: a gallery of drawings, and several rooms reserved exclusively for the works of local artists; the " Arrageoise " room, dedicated to local history (plan in relief of Arras, made in 1715, from an original design in the Musée des Invalides, Paris; plans of the town at various periods; a series of pictures touching the story of the " Holy Candle "; fine old tapestries and lace of local manufacture; ceramic, numismatic and natural history collections, etc.

WOMAN'S HEAD (*14th Century*).

After visiting the ruins of the Palais St. Vaast, return to the Place de la Madeleine.

To the right of the Palais, take the Rue des Murs-St. Vaast, at the

THE PALAIS ST. VAAST.
The Peristyle of the Grand Cloister leading to the Cathedral.

end of which, turn left into the Rue Méaulens. The façade of the north transept of the cathedral, in front of the ruins of which the tourist passes (*see* **drawing**, *p.* 49), **stood** *in this street. The Rue Méaulens was amongst those which suffered most from the bombardments.*

*Turn into the Rue des Teinturiers (first on the left), which skirts the main façade of the Cathedral (**see map**, p. 42).*

General View of the Cathedral.

The Cathedral.

The beautiful original Gothic Cathedral of Arras, erected in the 12th and 13th centuries, having been first sold as national property, then pulled down during the Revolution, the church of St. Vaast Abbey became the Mother-Church in the 19th century.

The Collapse of the North Transept.
Drawing by A. Ventre, chief architect to the Historical Monuments Department.

The new cathedral, now entirely in ruins, was a very large building, the erection of which was begun in 1755 from plans by Coutant d'Ivry, the architect who, later, built the Church of La Madeleine in Paris. The work was interrupted during the Revolution, then resumed by virtue of a municipal decree dated "Nivôse 27, Year XII", which ran: "*...to erect the edifice, abandoning everything in the original plans connected with decoration and architectural beauty, limiting the work to the requirements of solidity and decency.*" The church was finished in accordance with these prescriptions, being completed in 1834. The interior was of plaster-

The Interior of the Cathedral.

coated brickwork, whilst the columns were of undressed stone, covered with stone-coloured mortar. The capitals were of stucco-work.

Built in the shape of a Latin cross, the Church measured 330 feet in length, 86 feet in width and 106 feet in height. It comprised a great four-bayed nave with side-aisles, a wide double transept, a two-bayed choir, and an apse with ambulatory, off which opened seven chapels.

The main (west) façade has retained its principal lines. In front is a flight of 48 stone steps, with four landings, the three entrance-doors being almost on a level with the roofs of the surrounding houses. Built in the style of the Jesuits, it comprises two superimposed stories, one with eight, the other with four composite capitaled columns, the whole terminating in a triangular pediment.

Today, the cathedral forms one of the most impressive ruins of the war. As previously seen, from the Rue Méaulens, the façade of the north transept was entirely destroyed. One of the lateral bays of this transept, completely isolated, is still standing by a sheer miracle, without any support or vaulting (*photo p.* 49). The roof and framework of the entire building fell down after the fire of July 1915.

16TH CENTURY TRIPTYCH : THE MIRACLE OF THE HOLY CANDLE (*See p.* 56).
In the centre is seen the ancient Gothic Cathedral.

In the great nave, transept and choir, the semi-circular vaulting also collapsed. On the other hand, most of the columns with Corinthian capitals are still standing, either alone, or supporting the fragments of vaulting which still cover the side-aisles.

16TH CENTURY TRIPTYCH : THE CRUCIFIXION.

15TH CENTURY HEAD OF CHRIST, IN CARVED WOOD.

The great absidal chapel, or Chapel of the Virgin, is the least damaged part of the Cathedral. It is covered with a cupola, ornamented with frescoes. The latter, similar in design to those in the *Capella Borghese* of the *Santa Maria Maggiore* in Rome, represent The Glorification of the Virgin.

The Cathedral contained a number of interesting art treasures, which were fortunately saved. Among them are:

Two triptychs of the Flemish School of the 16th century, painted by Jehan Bellegambe of Douai, one representing "*Christ and his executioners*" (*photo*; *p.* 51), the other, "*Worshipping the Child Jesus*"; another 16th century triptych: "*The Miracle of the Holy Candle of Arras*", with an interesting view of the ancient Gothic Cathedral (*photo p.* 51); a painting attributed to Rubens: "*The Descent from the Cross*"; two paintings attributed to Van Dyck: "*The Entombment*" and "*The Death of Christ*"; a painting attributed to Ribéra: "*The Virgin, and Donors*"; a painting by Van Thulden: "*The Invocation of St. Bernard*"; two other paintings of the 16th century Flemish School: "*The Martyrdom of St Ursula and the* 11,000 *Virgins*" and "*Christ, the Victor*"; a fine 15th century "*Head of Christ Crucified*", in carved oak, taken from an old "calvary" at Arras (*photo above*); a small bas-relief in chased and gilt copper, dating from the end of the 16th century: "*The Legend of St. Eloi*"; a statue of "*The Virgin*", by Cortot (1843); tombstone and statue of *Philippe Coverel*, Abbot of St. Vaast, who died in 1636; 17th century marble statues of *Philippe de Tarcy*, Governor of Arras, and his wife, etc.

The Treasure included fragments of the heads of St. James the Greater and St. Léger, the bodies of St. Vaast and Saints Ranulphe and Radulphe, and the blood-stained surplice worn by Thomas à Becket at the time of his assassination.

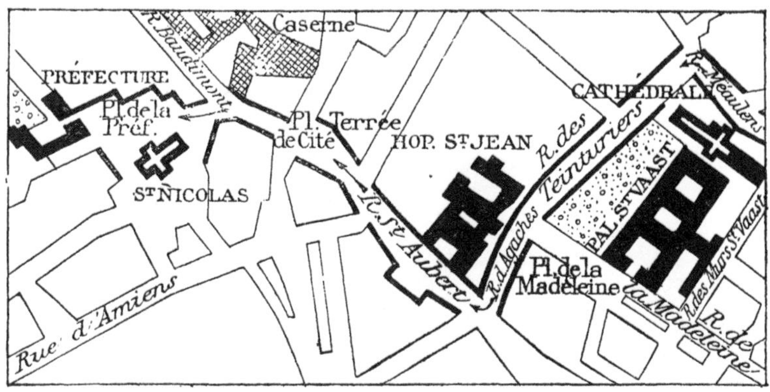

FROM THE CATHEDRAL TO THE PREFECTURE.
Follow the roads shown by thick lines.

After visiting the Cathedral, take the Rue des Teinturiers and the Rue des Agaches to the main thoroughfare of Arras, which at that point is called the Rue St. Aubert. The tourist soon reaches the small Place du Wetz-d'Amain, on the right of which are the spacious buildings of the ST. JOHN'S HOSPITAL.

The foundation of this hospital goes back to the time when Arras belonged to the Counts of Flanders. It was entirely rebuilt in the 19th century. During the early bombardments, it was struck by several shells, several of the inmates and nurses being among the victims.

At the opposite end of the Place du Wetz-d'Amain, are the remains of the ancient HOTEL DE CHAULNES, a turretted fortress built in the Middle Ages, and enlarged and considerably modified in the 16th century.

THE ST. JOHN HOSPITAL. ONE OF THE WARDS.

BAUDIMONT GATE.

During the wars of the 15th century, this ancient fortress, with its thick walls and vaulting, was used by the Abbots of Mont St. Eloi as a refuge for the monks of their brotherhood. With the exception of the roof, these ruins suffered little damage from the German guns.

The Rue St. Aubert ends at the small Terrée-de-Cité square, so called because it was built on the site of the old city ramparts. In it is a Fountain of Neptune. The Rue Baudimont prolongs the Rue St. Aubert, beyond the Place Terrée-de-Cité, and ends 500 *yards further on at the* BAUDIMONT GATE. Rebuilt in 1863, it was the only gate remaining of the seven which formerly gave access to the fortified city (*photo above*).

Keep along the Rue Baudimont as far as the Place de la Préfecture, on the left. This square, situated on the top of the hill, occupied the site of the mediæval *Cité*, i. e. of that part of Arras which was placed under the Bishop's authority.

In the middle of the square stands the CHURCH OF ST NICOLAS, built in the Neo-Greek style, in 1846, on the site of the old Gothic Cathedral of Arras, which was destroyed during the Revolution.

Preceded by a large peristyle with Ionic columns, the vital portions of the church are still standing. Among other interesting works of art, some of which came from the old Cathedral, are the following: finely carved confessionals, dating from the 16th century; the 13th century phylactery shrine of St. Nicholas' Tooth, in gilt copper and silver; a 16th century reliquary bust of St. Lambert, in gilt copper; the folding leaves of two triptychs — painted pannels, dating from late 16th century — representing *The Carrying of the Cross, The Entombment, The Virgin and Child, the donor, and the Fathers of the Latin Church;* an early 18th century painting, depicting a symbolical procession.

Skirt St. Nicholas' Church, on the right. At the bottom of the square is the entrance to the Préfecture, whose buildings occupy the site of the ancient Palace of the Bishop of Arras, Lord of the *Cité*.

Behind the Préfecture (seriously damaged), is an immense park with fine plantations, which were partly ravaged by shell-fire.

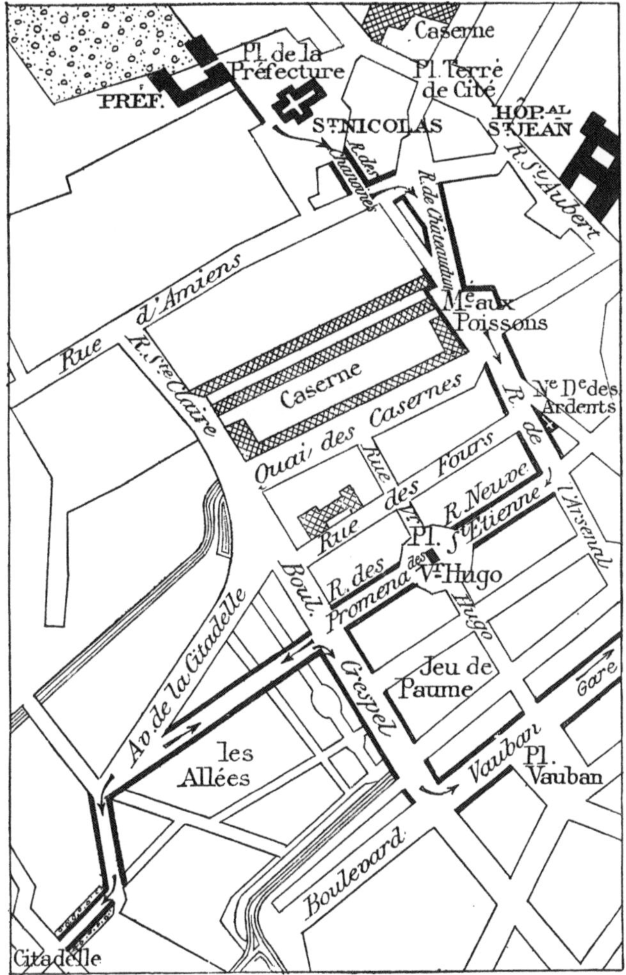

From the Prefecture to the Station, via the Citadelle
Follow the roads shown by thick lines.

Having passed in front of the Préfecture, go round the chevet of St. Nicholas' Church, and take the short Rue des Chanoines which descends, on the right, towards the Rue d'Amiens.

Take the Rue d'Amiens, on the left, and turn into the second street on the right (Rue de Châteaudun).

Follow the latter to a small square, on the left of which is the Fishmarket, *and on the right, the* City Barracks (*18th century*).

Keep straight on, then take the Rue de l'Arsenal, to the Church of Notre-Dame-des-Ardents.

THE CHURCH OF NOTRE-DAME-DES-ARDENTS. THE CHEVET.

Notre-Dame-des-Ardents Church was somewhat damaged by the bombardments. It was built about 1880, to commemorate the miraculous cure of the " Mal des Ardents ", with which Arras was stricken in the Middle Ages. According to tradition, this plague was stamped out through the intervention of the Virgin. Two itinerant fiddlers received a candle, a few burning drops from which, spilt on the stricken people, sufficed to cure them (*See pp.* 33 *and* 51).

The Church possesses a 13th century shrine of chased silver, containing fragments of the " Holy Candle ".

Keep along the Rue de l'Arsenal, as far as the Rue Neuve-St-Etienne, which take on the right. The COLLÈGE, housed in an 18th century mansion, *is passed on the left, at the corner of the two streets.*

THE PLACE VICTOR-HUGO.

THE PROMENADE LEADING TO THE CITADELLE.

The Rue Neuve-St-Etienne leads to the PLACE VICTOR-HUGO, *in which stands* a Pyramid (now truncated) dating from 1779. Octagonal in shape, the Place Victor-Hugo stands in the centre of this quarter of the city, the streets of which are straight, and intersect one another at right angles. This part of the city was built in the 18th century, and was then known as the " Basse Ville " or Lower Town.

Beyond the Place Victor-Hugo, take the Rue des Promenades as far as the Boulevard Crespel (*see map, p. 55*).

The Boulevard Crespel runs alongside the fine PROMENADE DES ALLÉES which, planted with century-old lime-trees and elms, separates the Lower Town from the Citadelle.

Turn left into the Boulevard Crespel, unless it is desired to visit the Citadelle, in which case, go straight along the avenue which prolongs the Rue des Promenades. At the end of the avenue, turn left, to reach the entrance to the Citadelle. Return by the same way to the Boulevard Crespel.

THE CITADELLE.

THE CITADELLE CHAPEL.

The Citadelle.

The Citadelle was built in 1670-1674, from plans by Vauban.

Fearing a survival of the memories left behind by the Spanish occupation, Louis XIV had this fortress built to keep the people of Arras in check. When it was completed, Vauban wrote to Louvois : " *It will effectually dominate the town, enfilade many streets and demolish the buildings* ". But although the Citadelle could subdue rebellions inside the town, it was ineffectual against an enemy from the outside, and soon came to be known as " The Useless Beauty ".

In shape a pentagon, the Citadelle was commanded by five bastions, originally known as the King, Queen, Dauphin, Orléans and Anjou. These bastions, with their powerful walls and outer moat, are protected by five semi-circular advance-works connected together by curtains. Two gates looking, the one towards the town and the other towards the country (formerly the " Royal Gate " and " Succour Gate ") give access to the Citadelle (*photo, p.* 57).

Inside, is the CITADELLE CHAPEL, a graceful 17th century structure with colonnaded stories surmounted by a round pediment and a campanile (*photo above*).

The Boulevard Crespel leads to the Boulevard Vauban, which take on the left. Pass the small Place Vauban, on the left, to the Hagerue cross-roads reached shortly afterwards. Here, take the Boulevard Carnot, on the right, back to the Place de la Gare.

A VISIT TO THE BATTLEFIELDS OF ARTOIS.

(*Map below,* 31 *kms.*)

a) **From Arras to Mont-Saint-Éloi** (*Map No.* 2, *below*; 9 *kms.*).

Leave Arras by the Rue de Lille, Rue de Lens and Faubourg St Catherine. After crossing the Scarpe, **St Catherine** *is reached.*

Leave the Béthune (*N.* 37) *and Lille* (*N.* 25) *roads, on the right, taking that on the left to St-Eloi* (*G. C.* 52), *here called the Chaussée Brunehaut. This is an old Roman causeway and runs in a perfectly straight line.*

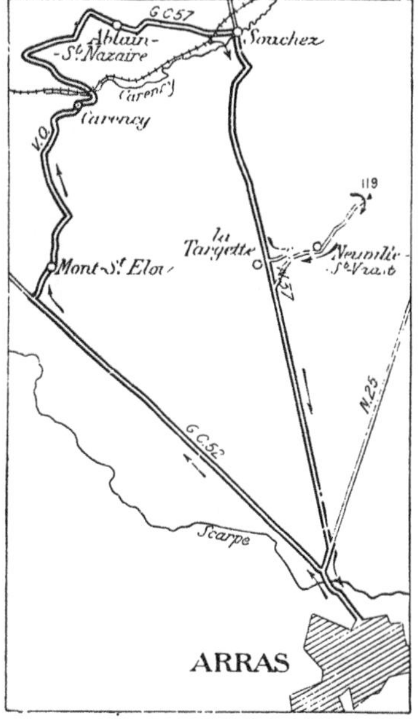

ITINERARY, NORTH OF ARRAS.

Mont-St.-Éloi.

After passing through Anzin-St Aubin, the ruins of two high towers, truncated and torn by the shells, will be noticed on the left. From same, there is a magnificent view of the surrounding country.

These towers are the last remaining vestiges of a famous abbey founded by St. Eloi in the 7th century and which was the centre of many stirring events. Several battles were fought under its walls.

In 1477, Louis XI, who was then besieging Arras, established himself there with his army. Two centuries later (1654) Condé made the place his headquarters, but was driven out by the troops under Turenne.

The Abbey was several times destroyed during these wars, but was always restored. In the middle of the 18th century, it was entirely rebuilt, but the work was scarcely completed, when the Revolution broke out. The Abbey was first secularized and sold as national property, then pulled down, with the exception of a monumental gate and the towers of the abbey church façade.

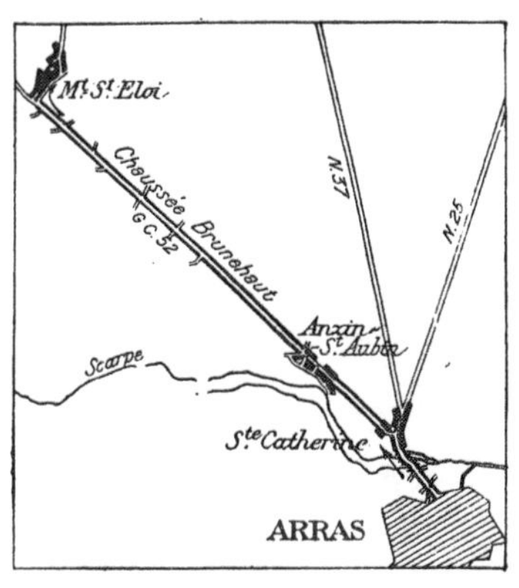

FROM ARRAS TO MONT-ST. ELOI (9 kms).

The towers were severely damaged during the war, but although now in ruins, their aspect is still imposing. They overlook the village of Mont-St-Eloi, which also suffered severely from the bombardments (*photos, pp.* 60-62).

PANORAMA, SEEN FROM ONE OF THE TOWE

Mont-Saint-Eloi was a first-rate Observation-Post, commanding as it did the the whole of the battlefields of Artois.
Two long spurs shut in the horizon, on the north-east:
Notre-Dame-de-Lorette (on the left) and Vimy Ridge (on the right).

To reach the towers, leave the Chaussée Brunehaut, and take the steep paved street on the right (photo below). After crossing through the village, the tourist arrives at the towers (altitude: 400 feet).

CROSSING OF THE CHAUSSÉE BRUNEHAUT WITH THE ROAD TO THE ABBEY OF MONT-ST-ELOI.

Originally about 175 feet in height, each tower comprised four square storeys, decorated with the classical Doric, Ionic and Corinthian columns. Nearly the whole of the upper portion of the towers has fallen down.

Between the towers may be seen the remains of the entrance-portal, surmounted by an interior gallery of the old abbey church.

...OF MONT-ST-ELOI ABBEY.

Between the two spurs is a narrow pass, through which flows the River Souchez. A road, leading to Lens, runs alongside the river. From here, one readily grasps the aim of the Artois Offensives, by which the Allies sought to drive the enemy from the dominating crests, and to reach the Plain of Lens, through the Souchez Pass.

THE ABBEY TOWERS, SEEN FROM THE OBSERVATION-POST IN THE ABBEY FARM.

The Towers of Mont-St-Eloi Abbey.

Tourists may go up the right-hand tower. Enter by the interior breach, the upper part of which is visible in the photo, behind the fragment of enclosure wall.

To ascend the right-hand tower (photo above) enter same from the rear. After climbing 104 steps, a small door on the right leads to a platform, which cross, to reach a gap, through which there is an extensive view of the surrounding country.

b) **From Mont-St-Eloi to Carency.** (*See maps below, 4 kms*).

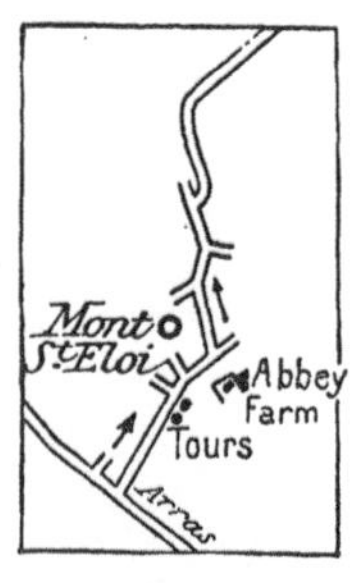

Mont-Saint-Eloi.

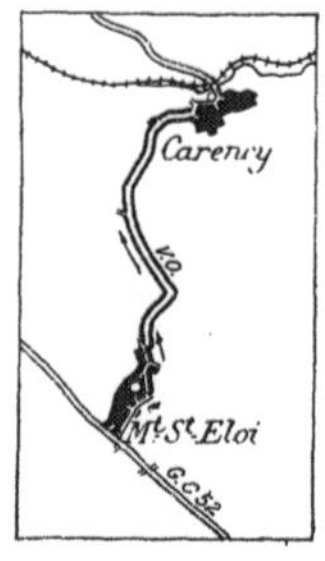

From Mont-St-Eloi to Carency.

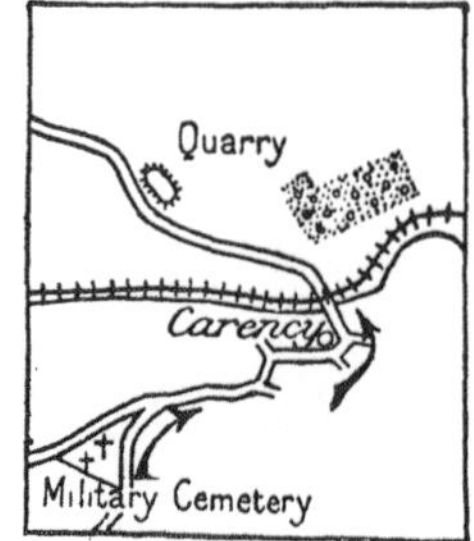

Carency.

After descending the tower, continue along the street, then take the first turning on the left, opposite the Abbey Farm. The street dips

French Cemetery at the entrance to Carency.
(*See sketch-map No. 3, page 62*).

down to the village. Outside the latter, at the cross-roads, take the right-hand road in the direction of Carency.

1,500 *yards beyond Mont-St-Eloi, there is a sunken by-road, to the right of the main road, alongside which is a large French military cemetery.* 2 *kms. further on, at the entrance to Carency, there is another cemetery on the left of the road (photo above).*

Carency.

The village of Carency lies along the slopes of a narrow valley, at the bottom of which runs the Carency Stream. The latter shortly afterwards becomes the Souchez (at Lens), then the Deule (at Lille). To the north of the brook runs the single-gauge Frévent-Lens railway.

The village comprised five groups of houses: one in the centre, which included the Church, and the other four facing the four cardinal points. Starting from the eastern group there is a road which leads to Souchez, bounded on the north by the wood and brook of Carency, and on the south by ravines.

The position of Carency had been in the enemy's hands since October 1914, and formed a salient in their lines. Connected up with their general defences by trenches and boyaux on each side of the Carency-Souchez road, it formed a strategic position of great importance for the Germans, preventing as it did any French advance towards Lens, or direct communication between Arras and Béthune.

The village had accordingly been transformed into an almost impregnable fortress, defended by four lines of trenches. Each street and house was fortified, subterranean passages connecting up the cellars. In the gardens which surrounded the houses, were numerous batteries of artillery and countless machine-guns. The garrison consisted of four battalions and at least six companies of engineers, under the command of a brigadier-general.

As early as December 1914, the French attempted to take Carency. Two attacks on the 18th and 27th of that month, advanced their first lines to the northern and western outskirts of the village, but further progress was stayed by violent machine-gun fire.

Then began a long period of raids and mining operations, which continued throughout the Winter, until the Spring. Over a hundred mines were sprung. Little by little, the German trenches were destroyed, together with their deadly flanking positions, which bristled with machine-guns. Thus the French first lines were steadily brought closer to those of the enemy.

FORTIFIED HOUSES AT THE FOOT OF CARENCY CHURCH, IN MAY 1915.

In the course of these combats, the French generally remained masters of the edges of the craters, which they immediately organized defensively. In spite of the mud, into which the men sank up to their middle (1), they managed to hold them, despite the enemy's counter-attacks. Making sudden rushes from the cellars in the village, the Germans attempted to break the grip which was gradually strangling them. More than 2,700 yards of mine galleries were thus patiently bored and fired, until the enemy's positions were surrounded by an endless chain of mine craters, resulting in such a chaotic upheaval of the ground on the western flank of the village, that it became impossible to advance further on that side.

The attack of **May 9, 1915,** was therefore directed against the south-

---

(1) Rain fell continuously throughout the Winter, so that in January there was as much as 4 feet of water in some of the trenches.

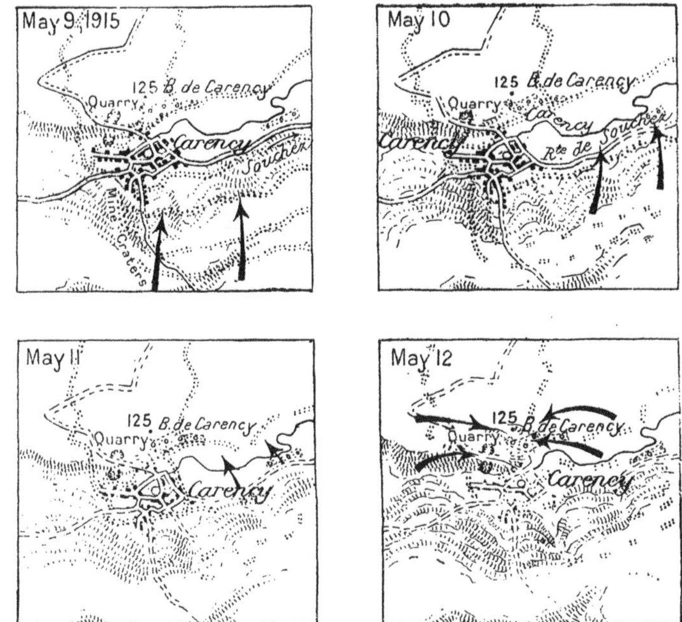

THE CAPTURE OF CARENCY.

Access to the village from the west being impossible on account of the mine craters, the attack began on the south, continued on the east, and ended on the northern side.

ern and eastern outskirts of the village. It was led by General Fayolle, who at that time was commanding a division of the 33rd Corps, then under the orders of General Pétain.

A series of strongly fortified ravines and hollows separated the French trenches from the southern outskirts of Carency, and from the Carency-Souchez road. In a single rush, the infantry covered the intervening ground, overcoming all obstacles and carrying three lines of trenches. However, having once reached the outskirts of the village, they had to conquer the ground, foot by foot, with grenades. By evening, the ruins of the southern group of houses were being hard pressed, and in places the first French trenches had almost reached the Carency-Souchez road.

The next day **(May 10)**, the investment continued on the east. The Souchez road was everywhere reached, and the enemy, unable to use the trenches along this road, were deprived of all means of communication with Souchez.

On **May 11**, the road was passed, and Carency Wood carried.

Finally, on the **12th**, the French captured the wooded hillock to the north-east of the village, known as Hill 125, whilst to the north-west, they captured an immense deep quarry, transformed into a fortified redoubt, against which the mining operations had proved ineffectual.

Carency was now totally invested. No longer able to retreat, the Germans were compelled to surrender. Waving their handkerchiefs

THE RUINS OF CARENCY CHURCH.

and raising their hands above the parapets, more than a thousand prisoners — Saxon infantry, Bavarian Chasseurs and Baden Guards, headed by a colonel — were soon hurrying along the trenches to the rear.

Not a single house in Carency escaped the devastating effect of the heavy artillery, first of the French, and afterwards of the Germans, whose shells continued for months to fall in the village.

The destruction was complete. As early as May 1915, when the French made their entrance, all the houses were ripped open from top to bottom, the very cellars being crushed in.

Here and there, a few deep underground shelters withstood the pounding, and these were used to shelter the garrison from the volleys of artillery fire which the Germans afterwards continued to direct against the village.

MINE CRATERS ON THE SOUTHERN CREST OF CARENCY.
The photo shows the German Shelters, half destroyed by French mines, on the day of the Attack (May 9, 1915).

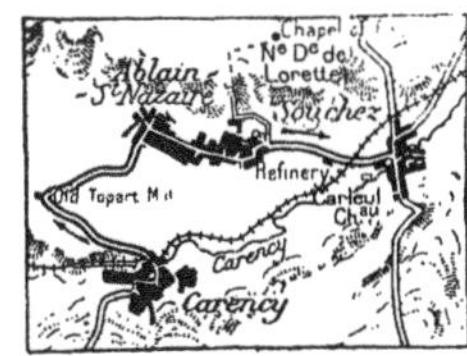

FROM CARENCY TO SOUCHEZ.

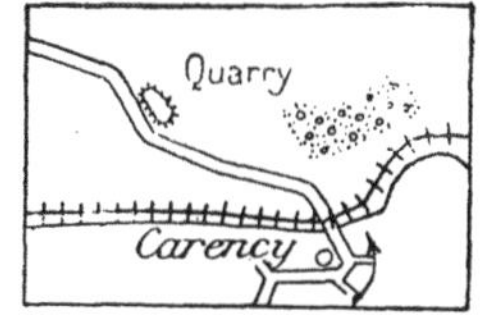

EXIT FROM CARENCY.

c) **From Carency to Souchez** (*see left-hand*[1] *sketch above*, 6½ *kms.*).

At the foot of the ruined church, take the road which crosses the valley of Carency, stopping the car on the opposite side, beyond the quarries. (*See the right-hand sketch above*).

From this dominating point, one gets a fine panoramic view of the village, and of the principal objectives of the attacks of May 1915. The crest opposite formed the line of departure of the attacking troops. On the right, in the western outskirts of the village, can be seen the field of mine craters. The crest on which the tourist is standing, was the final objective of the converging attacks which encircled Carency, (*see p.* 65).

TOPART MILL.

1½ *kms. beyond Carency*, the old TOPART MILL is passed (*photo above*). It stands on Hill 136, which was carried in a brilliant attack at the beginning of the Offensive of May 1915.

After passing Topart Mill and crossing the hill which separates the valley of the Carency from that of the St. Nazaire, the road descends to **Ablain-St-Nazaire.** *It was from there that the panorama on pages* 68-69 *was taken.*

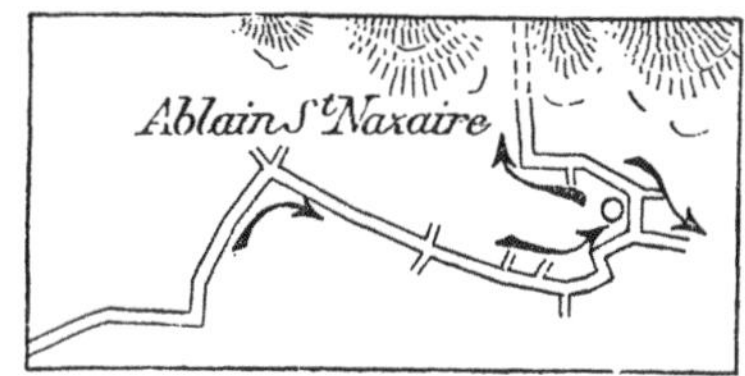

ABLAIN-SAINT-NAZAIRE.

Panorama of the Battlefields...

The Church of Ablain-St-Nazaire in 1919.

ABLAIN-SAINT-NAZAIRE.

Keeping along the road, Ablain-St-Nazaire (totally destroyed) *is entered from the south-west.* Its shapeless ruins extend for nearly a mile on both sides of the St. Nazaire stream.

The village was powerfully fortified by the Germans. Each group of houses formed a centre of resistance, held by a strong garrison and defended by large numbers of machine-guns. Its capture was consequently long and arduous.

Begun immediately after the fall of Carency (May 12), it was completed only on May 29, by the capture of a large block of houses, which prolonged the burgh to the north, towards the slopes of

.DE-LORETTE —— VIMY RIDGE. ——

Blanche Voie Spur. Souchez Spur. Ablain Church. Souchez Pass. Carleul Park. The Pimple. Hill 119. N. 37. Arras-Bethune. Hill 140. Folie Farm.

.OF ARTOIS (*see pages* 71-75).

Notre-Dame-de-Lorette.

The village of Ablain-St-Nazaire possessed a church of great historical interest.

It was built at the beginning of the 16th century, in 15th century Gothic style, by the lord of Carency and the nobles of Artois.

On the western façade rose a large square tower, 114 feet high, flanked by massive buttresses and surmounted by a battlemented parapet with watch - towers at the corners.

THE CHURCH OF ABLAIN-ST-NAZAIRE BEFORE THE WAR (*Hist. Mon.*).

General View of Ablain-St-Nazaire, as seen from N.-D.-de-Lorette.

The great portal of the south façade, ornamented with exceptionally fine sculpture, was one of the most remarkable in the whole region.

Ablain-St-Nazaire and the Spur of Notre-Dame-de-Lorette.

THE SPUR OF NOTRE-DAME-DE-LORETTE.
The road becomes impracticable at the point where the car is standing.

NOTRE-DAME-DE-LORETTE.

Ablain-St-Nazaire is dominated on the north by the crest of Notre-Dame-de-Lorette. *A road starting near the church leads to the place where, on Hill* 165, *stood a chapel of that name. Take this road for* 500 *yards, at which point it becomes impracticable for cars. Continue on foot, to visit the Massif of Lorette.*

From the spot where the car is left, the path on the left which leads up to the crest, in the direction of the chapel, can be followed with the eye (see photo above). Further to the right, a boyau leads thither in an almost straight line, crossed, near the top, by a trench. This trench runs to the right, towards the eastern slope of the massif, whence the finest panoramic view of the battlefields is to be obtained.

Ascend by the path leading to the site of the chapel, returning by the boyau, after visiting the plateau and admiring the panorama.

The top of Notre-Dame-de-Lorette forms a long spur, which, extending west to east, from Bouvigny Wood to the north of Souchez, advances as a promontory into the Plain of Lens, as far as the outskirts of the coal district. At the top of the eastern portion, near a point shown on the map as " Cote 165 ", there stood, before the war, the Chapel of Notre-Dame-de-Lorette, a popular local pilgrimage.

Whilst the northern slopes of the plateau are fairly gentle, those on the reverse side are very steep. Five abrupt counterscarps, separated by narrow ravines, run from the massif to the south-east. Seen from the depression of Ablain-St-Nazaire, they somewhat resemble the sections of a melon, and were accordingly christened " Côtes de Melon " by the *poilus*. Considered from west to east, they are the Mathis Spur, Grand Spur, Arabes Spur, Blanche-Voie Spur and Souchez Spur, which latter towers above the eastern exit from Ablain-St-Nazaire and the sugar-refinery situated on the Souchez road. (*Sketch, p.* 72).

From the beginning of the trench warfare period, the French 10th Army attempted to carry this position.

In December 1914 and January 1915, the 21st Corps, under the command of General Maistre, gained a footing on the Mathis Spur. On March 15, 1915, after most violent fighting, they carried the next (Grand) Spur, defended by three successive lines of trenches, and held it, in spite of powerful counter-attacks, which often degenerated into

THE ATTACK ON N.-D.-DE-LORETTE CREST.
It broke down against the Chapel Fortress.

furious hand-to-hand struggles. In the following month the third (Arabes) Spur was carried.

After these preliminary attacks, the Artois Offensive was launched on May 9. The 21st Corps received orders to drive the enemy from the last two spurs of the massif, and to carry the upper crest, on the eastern edge of which stood Lorette Chapel, separated from the first French trenches by some 1,000 yards.

The German defences were truly formidable. From Arabes Spur to the Souchez-Aix-Noulette road (N. 37), running at the foot of the north-eastern slopes of the hill, were echeloned five lines of deep trenches which for six months had been reinforced with sacks of earth and cement, and protected with double and triple lines of barbed wire and "chevaux-de-frise". Every 100 yards, barricades armed with machine-guns had been erected, forming powerful flanking positions. Several redoubts and advance-works served as points of support for the defence of the trenches. One of them, north-east of the chapel, comprising moats, palisades, casemates and shelters 35 or more feet in depth, prevented access to the end of the plateau.

A division of picked troops, mostly Baden men, had orders to hold Notre-Dame-de-Lorette at all cost, whilst in the rear, concealed in the large straggling villages of Angres and Liévin, powerful artillery swept the whole of the northern flank of the hill and the plateau itself with continuous fire (*see map, p.* 8).

General Maistre's Division, which had charge of the attack, comprised three infantry regiments and three battalions of Chasseurs.

On **May 9,** at 10 a. m., the first waves dashed forward. Two hours later, three lines of defences had been carried, and the key of the position — the chapel fortress — reached, where the German machine-gunners, behind heaps of earth-bags and thick steel-plates kept up a withering fire. The attack broke down against this formidable obstacle, the assailants suffering heavy casualties. Some of the companies, having lost all their officers, were commanded by sergeants. The advance was now effected by rushes from one shell-hole to another. Large areas of "chevaux-de-frise" situated in a depression of the ground in front of the fortress, were still practically intact. However, the Chasseurs would not give in. Although their ranks were terribly depleted, they clung to the ground and were soon joined by the infantry. The fighting continued furiously with grenade, bayonet and knife, the German machine-gunners firing the while uninterruptedly.

Night fell, lighted up by the shells and rockets, and torn by the cries of the wounded, the roar of the explosions, and the crackling of the machine-guns. Chasseurs and infantry improvised positions on the conquered ground. Before an enormous mine-crater ninety yards in circumference, they pushed the corpses to the bottom, and organised themselves on the edges, behind improvised parapets.

From **May 10 to 12,** the situation remained unchanged. The French fully maintained their gains, and even increased them slightly, while the German machine-guns fired without respite.

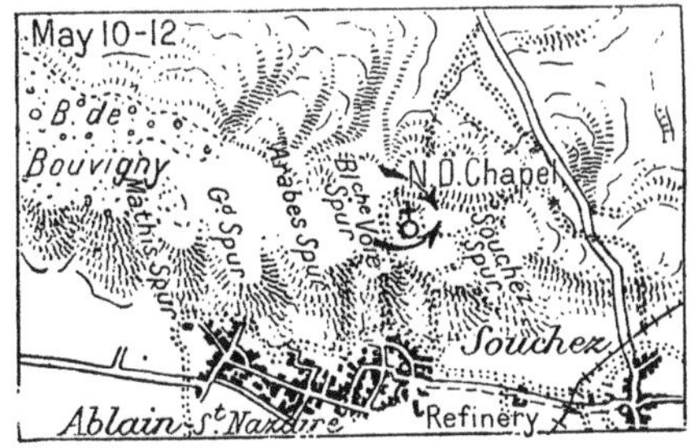

THE ATTACK ON N.-D.-DE-LORETTE CREST.
The capture of the Chapel.

" It is hot, and the smell is atrocious. The dead of the previous months, with only the thinnest covering of earth over them, have been torn from their graves by the shells. The plateau is a charnel-house..."

On May 12, at night-fall, the Chasseurs left their entrenchments, and throwing themselves flat on the ground, wriggled up to the fortress. There, below the machine-guns, which were firing about two feet above their heads, they wrenched out sacks of earth and thrust them into the loop holes, thereby slackening the enemy's fire. Taking advantage of the lull, the supports rushed up, and the wave swept over the parapet.

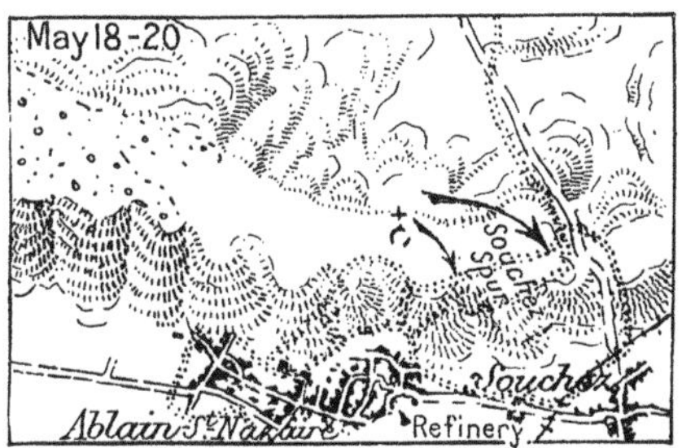

THE ATTACK ON N.-D.-DE-LORETTE CREST.
The French masters of the Crest.

Inside the fortress, furious hand-to-hand fighting followed in the pitch darkness. The Germans were beaten, and the chapel, in ruins, was left behind. Beyond, was an inextricable, chaotic tangle of underground passages and shelters, mine-craters, and shell-holes, encumbered with dead, arms, equipment and stores.

Although masters of the crest of the Plateau of Notre-Dame-de-Lorette, the French were not yet in possession of the whole massif, as the Germans were still holding the two spurs of Blanche-Voie and Souchez. The rain, added to the numerous springs to be found in the region, had transformed the clay soil into a swamp, which made any advance extremely difficult. However, Souchez Spur was gradually conquered on the following days, to the point where it looks down upon the sugar refinery at Souchez. On the other hand the enemy's galling machine-

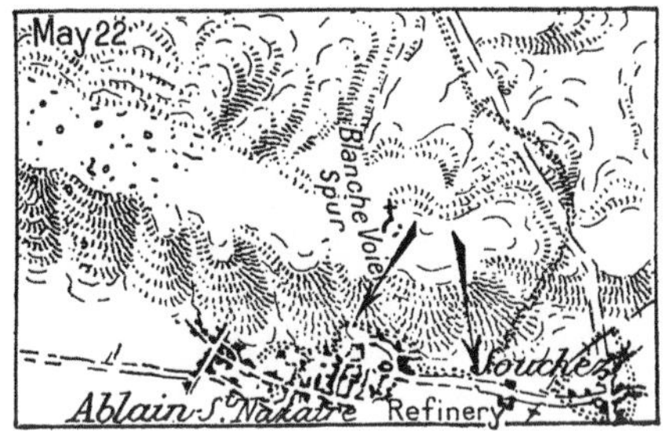

THE ATTACK ON N.-D.-DE-LORETTE CREST.
The entire massif of Lorette was taken.

NOTRE-DAME-DE-LORETTE CHAPEL IN 1914. (*See below*).

gun fire broke all attacks on the Blanche-Voie. Up to **May 20,** the French line described a wide semi-circle, from the west of Ablain-St-Nazaire to the flanks of the eastern spur, passing round the other counterscarp. For eight days more, the Germans, crouching in their entrenchments on the Blanche-Voie and in the houses which they still held to the north and east of Ablain, swept the French lines unceasingly with their machine-gun fire, whilst their batteries at Angres and Liévin kept the top of the plateau under shell-fire.

Finally, on **May 22,** after two days of furious fighting, the trenches of Blanche-Voie were carried, and the whole of the massif of Notre-

THE CHAPEL OF NOTRE-DAME-DE-LORETTE WAS ENTIRELY DESTROYED.
(*The photo on the next page shows how it looked in* 1919.)

Dame-de-Lorette, except the lower part of the slopes of Souchez Spur, was occupied by the French (*see 3rd sketch, p. 73*).

The fighting had lasted thirteen days. On both sides, the losses were very heavy. Three thousand German dead were counted.

DEBRIS OF NOTRE-DAME-DE-LORETTE CHAPEL.

On July 11, 1915, General d'Urbal, commanding the French 10th Army, mentioned the 21st Corps and the 48th and 58th Divisions in the Army Order of the Day, in the following terms: *Under the command of General Maistre, gave proof of a tenacity and devotion above all praise, in the course of repeated attacks carried out during several consecutive weeks, under intense bombardment, day and night, by the enemy's artillery.*

When coming from Ablain-St-Nazaire, the tourist, on reaching the

THE CEMETERY NEAR THE SUGAR REFINERY AT SOUCHEZ.

PANORAMA SEEN FROM...

crest of the massif of Notre-Dame-de-Lorette, sees a plateau absolutely devoid of any sign of life. The ground is a mere succession of shell-holes and mine-craters, with no interesting remains of the old German defences.

As to the Chapel, the stone foundations of one of the walls, marked by two shelters of corrugated iron, are all that is left to show the passer-by where it once stood. Three small statues found when the débris were cleared away, may now be seen in one of the shelters (*photo p.* 75).

About half-a-mile to the right, the eastern slope is reached, from which there is a fine, extensive panorama (*photo above*) *:* in the hollow, are the shapeless ruins of the church and houses of Ablain-St-Nazaire; behind, those of Carency, and in the distance, the broken towers of Mont-St-Eloi; on the left, Souchez and beyond, the thinly scattered poplar-trees along the Béthune-Arras road; still further to the left, in a depres-

THE RUINED SUGAR REFINERY AT SOUCHEZ.
In the background: Notre-Dame-de-Lorette; on the left: Ablain-St-Nazaire Church.

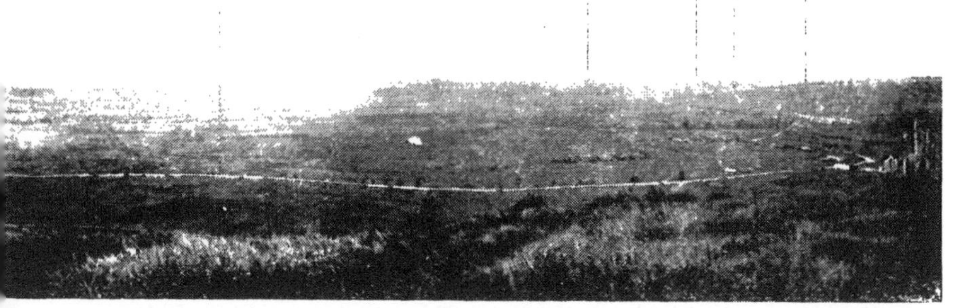

...NOTRE-DAME-DE-LORETTE.

sion of the ground, a confused mass of ruins : Angres, Liévin and Lens.

After visiting Notre-Dame-de-Lorette, return to Ablain-St-Nazaire ; in front of the church, take the Souchez road (see panorama above), which is bounded on the south by the St. Nazaire stream. Here, the ground, in a state of chaotic upheaval, presents an endless succession of shell-holes, many of which overlap one another.

About half-way on the road to Souchez, near a military cemetery (*photo p.* 75) is a heap of broken, battered vats rusting in the open—all that remains of the important SUGAR-REFINERY OF SOUCHEZ (*photo p.* 76). The Germans transformed the place into a formidable stronghold, to prevent any communication with Souchez. It was reached by the French on May 15, but was only carried on the 30th, after two days of bitter fighting. On the following night, the Germans succeeded in reoccupying the position, but were driven out for good at dawn.

CARLEUL CHATEAU PARK.

Furious counter-attacks by the enemy in June were broken, and only served to further increase their already heavy losses.

300 *yards beyond the sugar refinery, the western outskirts of Souchez are reached ; to the right of the road*, a few shell-torn trees stand out in the marshy, upturned ground. It was here that, before the War, the CHATEAU OF CARLEUL (modern) stood, built near the ruins of an ancient château, surrounded with water, in the centre of an immense park.

Souchez *is next entered.*

SOUCHEZ.

The village stands in a hollow, through which flow the St. Nazaire and Carency streams. These streams meet at Souchez, forming the river of that name. To the east, a gentle slope leads to Hill 119. The line of high ground continues thence towards the south-east, rising to an altitude of 460 feet. This, the famous Vimy Ridge, was the last obstacle barring the way to the Plain of Lens and Douai.

The Germans had made of Souchez a formidable stronghold. All the houses were fortified and armed with machine-guns. In the outskirts of the village was a series of strong-points : the Cabaret Rouge, the Cemetery, Souchez Wood, the Park and Castle of Carleul, and lastly, the embankment of the Frévent-Lens light railway, with the station of Ablain-Souchez at the western end of Carleul Park.

The fortified ruins of the castle were protected by an outer moat 16 feet wide, and the immense park formed the main bastion of the advanced defences. The ground was cut up in all directions with trenches and boyaux, protected by deep entanglements of barbed wire. Moreover, the whole park, and the wood which prolongs it to the east, had been turned into an immense swamp, by diverting the waters of the Carency Stream.

In the Spring of 1915, after the capture of Carency and the Sugar Refinery of Souchez, the French made several attacks on these de-

THE RUINS OF SOUCHEZ VILLAGE. *In the background : Givenchy Hill.*

THE STONE CROSS AT SOUCHEZ IN 1914.

fences, sometimes gaining a footing in the Park of the Château of Carleul, but each time their advance was checked by machine-gun fire, and they were compelled to relinquish the ground which they had conquered at heavy cost. The station, cemetery and Cabaret Rouge were likewise repeatedly attacked, but after frequently changing hands in June, the Germans were able to keep them.

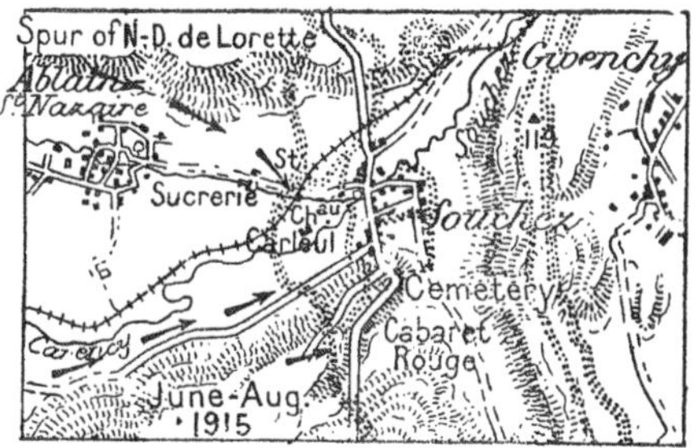

THE ABOVE CROSS IN 1919.

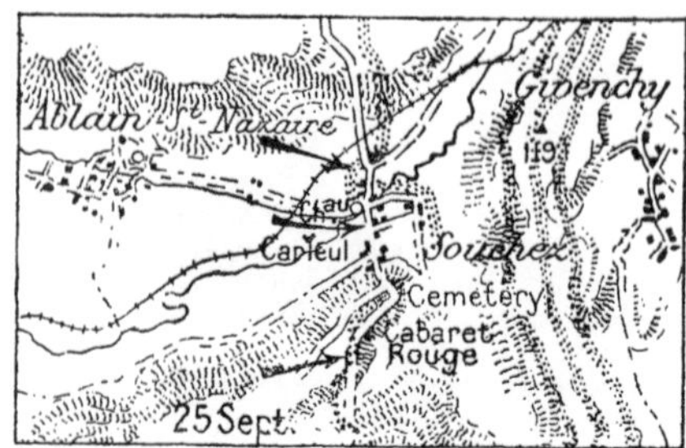

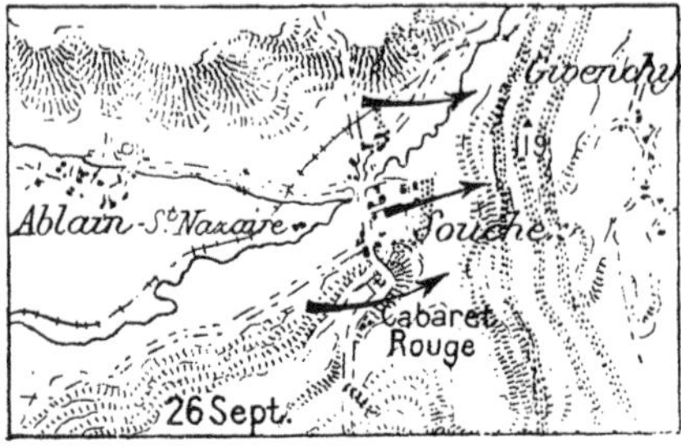

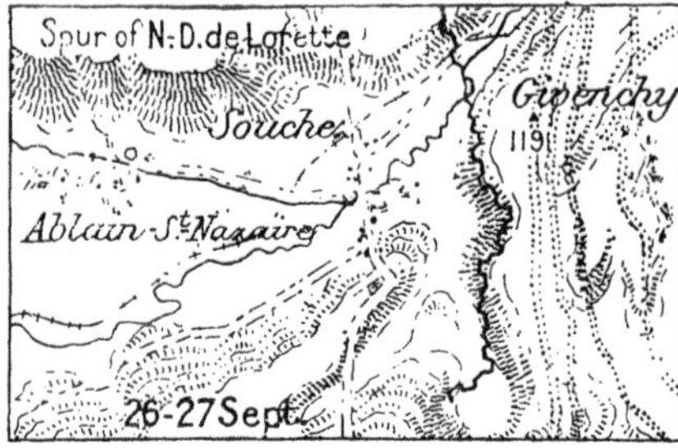

THE ATTACK AND CAPTURE OF SOUCHEZ.

Little by little, the opposing lines, separated by a few yards only, became fixed in the outskirts of Souchez, on either side of the Carency-Souchez railway. Fighting from trench to trench, with bombs and grenades, the struggle continued, without any appreciable result, and ended only with the Offensive of September.

On **Septembre 25,** after an artillery preparation lasting five days, a fresh general attack, directed by General Fayolle, was made against the village.

At the appointed time, the Chasseurs dashed across the railway which separated them from the Park of Carleul. By means of folding foot-bridges, they crossed the moats of the château, and entered the park. The Germans gave way under the violence of the shock, and a mad pursuit began over the muddy ground, across the swamps, mine-craters, labyrinth of trenches, fallen trees, etc... Souchez Wood was quickly reached, but from that point, the pursuit became more and more difficult, owing to the marshy ground which had been flooded by the Carency and St. Nazaire streams. Up to their knees — sometimes to their middle — in the water and mud, the Chasseurs nevertheless reached the approaches to the main road and church towards evening and strongly occupied the whole of the western outskirts.

Meanwhile, to the north, other units had captured the lines of trenches, north of the Ablain stream, and reached the northern outskirts of Souchez.

To the south, however, the attack was less successful. The cemetery, first carried by storm, had to be abandoned, and the flooded ground prevented any approach to the village in this direction.

On **September 26,** in the morning, the enemy were still holding the northern, southern and central portions of Souchez, and the situation was critical for the assailants. Large numbers of machine-guns kept up a deadly fire, whilst batteries posted in Angres, Liévin and

Givenchy enfiladed the depression of Souchez with incessant volleys of gas shells.

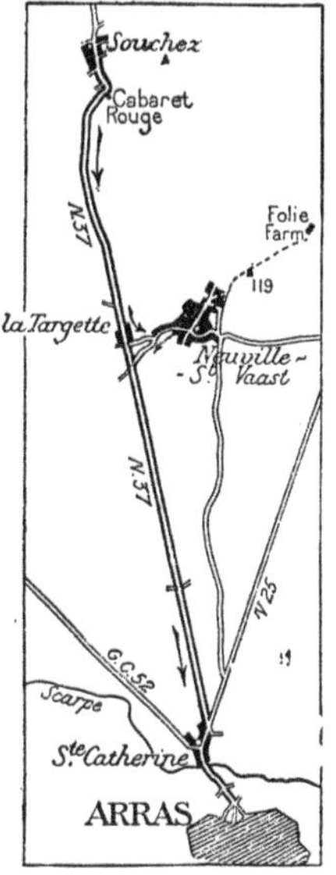

The French Commandant decided to make a frontal attack upon Souchez and to cross the village throughout its length, as far as the eastern outskirts. In spite of the stubborn resistance of the defenders, the houses, redoubts, and machine-gun nests fell one after the other. At night-fall, the French debouched from the village, and established their lines some 400 yards beyond the last houses on the eastern side of the village, along the road which runs at the foot of Hill 119.

Thus Souchez fell, 1,378 German prisoners being taken in two days; but of the once flourishing burgh, with its two railway-stations, large hospital, fine 15th century church (12th century spire), and famous 13th century stone cross, not a wall remains standing (*photos, pp.* 78-79).

d) **From Souchez to Arras** (*see map opposite*).

The road by which the tourist reaches Ablain-St-Nazaire ends at the central cross-roads of Souchez, in the middle of which stood a stone cross (*photos, p.* 79). *The site of this cross is marked by a heap of stones.*

Turn to the right, between the debris of the cross and the ruins of the church. The latter used to stand at the corner of the roads to Ablain and Arras. Take the Arras road (*N.* 37) *which, first straight, makes an " S " bend a short distance beyond the village.*

Hill 119 (*see map, p.* 82).

At the bend in the road, opposite the Cemetery of Souchez, *go on foot to* **Hill 119** (*about* 1 *km*). First a round hillock is crossed, alongside which runs the famous Chemin des Pylones, then through a field of shell-holes and old broken-down defences the tourist descends

Hill 119.

into Souchez Ravine. **Hill 119** rises steeply before us, and we see the torn tree stumps of Écouloirs Wood.

The slopes, at first very steep and crossed by horizontal banks, forming so many dark lines against the chalky background (*photo p.* 81), ease off towards a scarcely inclined *glacis* up to the line of the crest. The slopes were cut up by an inextricable labyrinth of boyaux and trenches, but the main line of resistance lay just behind the crest, on the counter-slope. Swept by the machine-guns of this line, the *glacis* was covered with deep entanglements of barbed-wire.

Hill 119 was carried in a single rush on May 9, 1915, and retaken by the Germans the same evening. Three fresh attacks by the French against this formidable position failed with heavy loss, in spite of the heroism of the men. It was finally conquered by the Canadians on April 10-11, 1917, after a terrible pounding by the artillery.

The Break-through of May 9, 1915.

On May 9, 1915, the 33rd Corps (Pétain), supported on the right by the 20th and on the left by the 21st, attacked from the southern outskirts of Carency and from Berthonval Wood, with the following objectives : the 70th Division (Fayolle), Carency; the 77th Division (Barbot), the Béthune road, then Carleul Park, Cabaret Rouge and Souchez Cemetery, one regiment to push on to Hill 119 and the village of Givenchy, whilst on the right, the Moroccan Division and the 20th Corps were to carry Hill 140, Folie Wood and Neuville-St-Vaast. Simultaneously, the 21st Corps, on the extreme left, after clearing the Crest of Notre-Dame-de-Lorette, had orders to turn Souchez from the north. (*See map, p.* 10).

At 5 a. m., on May 9, the troops were in their assigned positions. In perfect weather, the artillery preparation began at 6 a. m., the German guns replying but feebly.

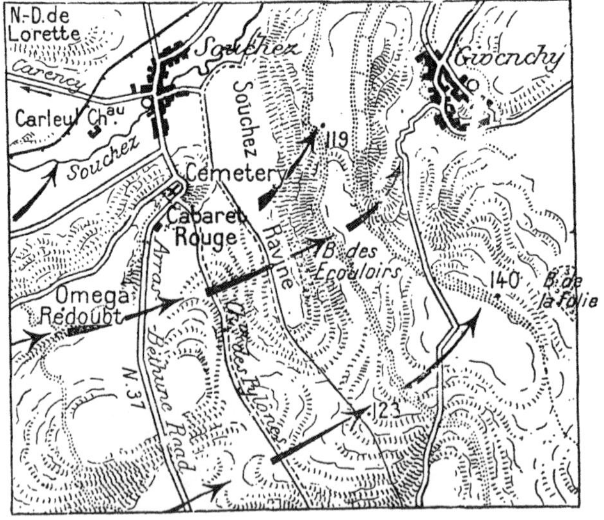

The attack on Hill 119 (May 9, 1915, *morning*).
The French gained a footing on Vimy Ridge.

" At 9.55 a. m., the bombardment doubles in intensity. The shells are falling like hail, the noise is infernal. Bayonets are fixed, the order " Forward " is given, the whole plain is alive... The great offensive has begun.

" To the yells of " En avant! En avant! ", the first line is carried. In many places, the Germans, half-dressed and stunned, have no time to resist. Elsewhere, they make a stubborn defence, and kill a lot of our men... But, no matter " En avant! "

" Now the Plain of Lens comes into sight, with its factories and countless red-roofed houses — the great city we are going to reconquer! The enormous wave sweeps madly onward. It is impossible to hold the men back for a moment, to bring them into something like order. Everyone runs, and how could we do otherwise, at the sight of the Germans, yonder, cutting it, for dear life, towards Carleul and Souchez?

" We are now in front of the famous OMEGA position, covered with barbed wire, almost intact. Through the rare gaps, the 97th and 159th enter together, and kill the defenders. Here, at last, is the Béthune road. Taking it, to the north, the 97th reach the Cabaret Rouge, carry the Cemetery of Souchez, and send out patrols into the heart of the village. It is 11 o'clock, and their mission is already fulfilled. Crossing the road, the 159th continue their advance towards Hill 119. Before them, opens the great Écouloirs Ravine, beyond which the cliffs of Hill 119 rise abruptly. Dashing in, the men discover and capture a battery of howitzers, around which they swarm, forming a human whirlpool of Alpine Chasseurs, Zouaves, Tirailleurs, extenuated with the charge, the heat, enthusiasm and thirst. " (Captain HUMBERT's *La Division Barbot.*)

On the right, veterans of the Foreign Legion, Tirailleurs and Zouaves of the Moroccan Division, attacked with the same ardour. Forc-

THE N. 37 (ARRAS-BÉTHUNE ROAD).
In the background : LA TARGETTE.

ing their way through the wire entanglements, which in places were still intact, they reached the second lines, leaving groups of men in front of the unconquered machine-guns. Trench-cleaners armed with grenades, revolvers and knives, carried the isolated strong points. In spite of the deadly machine-gun cross-fire from Neuville-St-Vaast, Folie Farm and Souchez, the enemy's resistance was vain. Reserves filled up the gaps in the ranks, and the wave of the storm troops swept up the slopes of the ridge, crushing all obstacles.

At 11.30 a. m., the Moroccan Division and the 159th Regiment reached the crest, whilst patrols entered Givenchy.

" We have broken through, and victory is ours. All hearts are filled with enthusiasm.

" Yes, the breach is open, but we cannot ask those who made it to go on. They are exhausted with fatigue, emotion, thirst, having advanced four and a half kilometres in an hour-and-a-half, which, in battle, is enormous. Then there is the question of our losses, until now unheeded. There are scarcely any officers left to lead the men ". (Captain HUMBERT's *La Division Barbot.*)

The reinforcements, so impatiently awaited, were long in coming. The advance had been too swift.

Supported by artillery, which they were able to bring up behind Folie Wood, the Germans counter-attacked in the afternoon, with fresh troops. The French African troops, exhausted and deprived of most of their officers, were overpowered, and the crest was retaken by the enemy.

From Hill 119, the Germans bombarded the plain with great violence.

" By evening, the cemetery nad become untenable, and had to be abandoned by the 97th, who took up positions 200 yards away, in

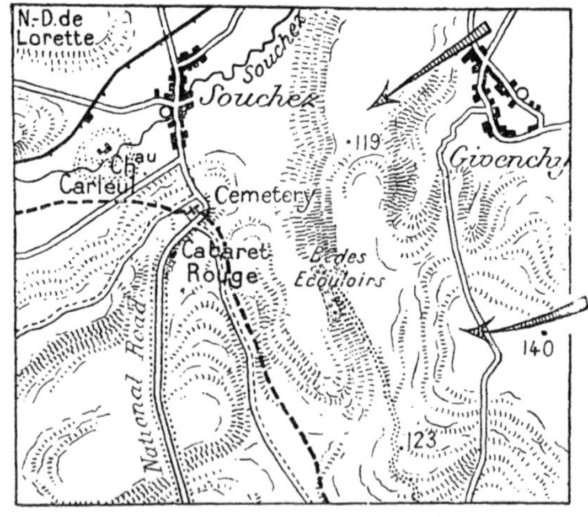

THE ATTACK ON HILL 119. (*May 9, 1915, evening*).
German Counter-Attacks forced the French to fall back on the Chemin des Pylônes and the Cabaret Rouge.

FOLIE WOOD. *On the skyline:* VIMY RIDGE.

front of the Cabaret Rouge. The 159th and the Moroccans established themselves near the Chemin des Pylônes. The Chasseurs held the road from Souchez to Carency, in the bottom of the valley. The Germans did not venture down Hill 119, to push home their advantage.

"Among all those who, that morning, had set out, confident of victory, and who, the same evening, were watching before Souchez, there was joy mingled with disappointment, but still great faith in the future."

The 70th Division having failed to capture Carency, and the 21st Corps being unable to debouch from Lorette, the offensive was checked.

"Temporarily seized with panic, the Germans quickly recovered. All their available reserves and artillery from the Artois, Picardy and Flanders fronts, were concentrated near Lens, in an effort to throw the French back on their departure bases."

VIMY RIDGE.

"The bombardment, accurately regulated from the top of Hill 119, increased, hour by hour.

" The trees along the Béthune road were gradually cut to pieces by the shells, and the Cabaret Rouge fell down.

" The survivors of the French attack, who had no time to dig themselves in deeply, lay on the ground, behind slight ridges of earth, which afforded little protection against the splinters. The number of the wounded increased with disconcerting rapidity, but they were forced to stay where they were, among the Tirailleurs, as the barrage prevented any movement being made to the rear.

" The field-kitchens could not reach the men, whose water-bottles were empty. The heat was suffocating on the arid plateau, and the men, mad with thirst, drank their own water..." (Captain HUMBERT's *La Division Barbot.*)

The Attack of June 16, 1915.

A new attempt having been decided on, the artillery was strongly reinforced, and enormous quantities of shells were accumulated near the batteries.

However, the Germans took similar measures, and replied to the French preparation with a still more violent counter-preparation.

The Moroccan Division were to attack Hill 119; the 77th Division, on their left, were to attack Souchez; the objective of the 9th Corps, on the right, was Hill 140.

The date and hour of the attack were fixed for June 16, at 12.15 p.m. In the centre, the 8th Zouaves and the 4th Tirailleurs opened the attack. Advancing swiftly through Souchez Ravine, the men scaled the abrupt slopes of Hill 119, carrying everything before them, except Écouloirs Wood — which they turned — and finally reached their objective.

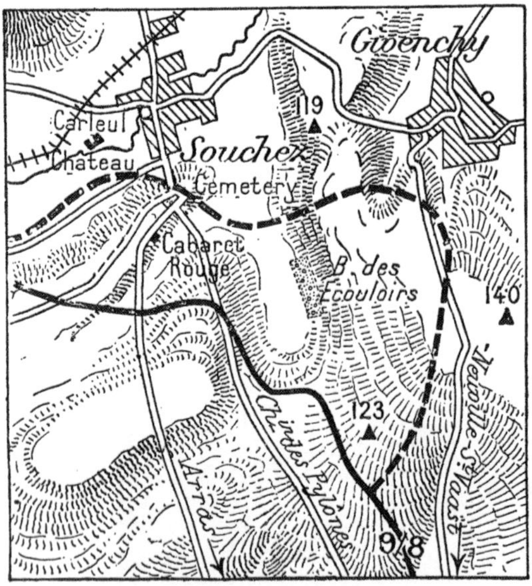

Less fortunate, the neighbouring divisions, on the right and left, were held by *rafales* of machine-gun fire, the 97th alone recapturing the cemetery. On the left flank of the 4th Tirailleurs, Souchez, forming a bastion, took the assailants, first in enfilade, then in the rear. One battalion was accordingly compelled to face towards Souchez, whilst the 8th Zouaves faced towards

THE ATTACK ON HILL 119, IN JUNE 1915.
The French advanced rapidly on June 16, but were driven back on the 22nd by Counter-Attacks.

Neuville-St-Vaast. The division's positions became fixed, describing a salient measuring some 2½ kilometres round its outer edge.

Against this wedge thus driven into their lines, the Germans launched repeated, unsuccessful counter-attacks. At 8 p. m., one of them, more powerful than the others, debouched from a sunken road, against the left of the line held by the Zouaves. One of the chaplains, his stick in one hand and his cap in the other, ran forward, shouting: "I may not shed blood, but I have my stick. Forward!" A group of Zouaves, galvanised by his words, charged the enemy and put them to flight.

Night fell. The position had to be held, and the 7th Tirailleurs of the Foreign Legion, reinforced the 8th Zouaves and 4th Tirailleurs.

The bombardment was such that it became necessary to relieve the Moroccan Division. The 60th and 61st Battalions of Chasseurs, with units from various other regiments, took their place in the "pocket", in which shells from Folie Wood, Givenchy Wood and Neuville-St-Vaast were falling thick and fast. To effect the relief and reach the new positions, the men had to cross the deep Souchez Ravine, which was being swept by the incessant fire of the machine-guns posted in Souchez and Écouloirs Wood. A boyau — the International Trench — crossed it, but the German 8in. shells levelled it as fast as the sappers of the division could make it.

On the 21st., the bombardment increased in fury. On the 22nd, at 2 a. m., the enemy launched a violent attack with an entire division. Thanks to the machine-gunners and also to the artillery-men, who for five days, in spite of fatigue, loss of sleep, the bombardment, and the bursting of some of their overworked guns, kept up a galling fire, it was thought for a moment that the German attack would fail.

However, the enemy had managed to slip in, at the base of the pocket, thereby threatening the communications between the French front and rear lines. To avoid a disaster, the danger had to be parried at once. The situation was critical, and the Zouaves were called for. Although they had only just been relieved, and had scarcely reached the rear, they returned at once to the front, with their leader, Colonel

THE CABARET ROUGE, ON THE N. 37.

Modelon. After a short preparation by a trench battery of 58's, they dashed forward. The enemy was held, and the pocket evacuated during the following night. Thus this new attack failed.

The sector — a hideous place, where the men, surrounded by rotting dead, lived in a pestilent atmosphere — was gradually organized.

The violence of the enemy's bombardment was maintained. Day and night, the 6in. and 8in. shells pounded the Cabaret Rouge, Souchez Cemetery and the Chemin des Pylônes.

From the crest, the enemy could see every movement of the French. It was only possible to move along the trenches at night. The wounded had to remain where they were until dark, with temporary dressings. Stretcher-bearers removed the dead under the cover of night.

On the night of July 12, a hail of gas shells fell on Souchez Cemetery, followed by an attack. In spite of a counter-attack by the 57th Battalion of Chasseurs, the cemetery was surrounded and lost.

The Operations during September 1915.

A general offensive was decided upon for the different fronts in Champagne, in conjunction with a feint attack in Artois.

Instead of repeating the furious bombardment of May 9, the cross-roads, trenches, organizations and houses were now subjected to a slow, carefully calculated pounding, with constant verifications as to range and effect. Instead of seeking to take the enemy by surprise, their positions were to be methodically destroyed. The preparation began on September 18.

The 77th Division were to carry Souchez, then cross Écouloirs Ravine and scale the Ridge, with the help of the 70th Division. To the north of Souchez, the 21st Corps were to attack the slopes of Lorette, towards Angres. On the south, the 3rd Corps (55th and 6th Divisions), in front of Neuville-St-Vaast, were to attack Hill 140 and Folie Farm.

The weather became uncertain. On the evening of the 24th, a violent storm transformed the trenches into ditches of mud. The men were wet through, and weighed down by the mud on their clothes and boots.

" On the 25th, the bombardment increased, but did not equal in intensity that of May 9. The enemy had devined our intentions, and for the past week had retaliated with 3, 6 and 8in. shells, which levelled the trenches and parallels of departure. In many places, the narrow boyaux were choked with dead.

" The bombardment grew more intense... At 12.15 p. m., the attack began.

" All the men " went over ", but it was no longer the fine human wall of May 9. The ground was in a terrible state of upheaval. Stumbling along, now floundering in the shell-holes, the men painfully made their way across the infernal chaotic waste. The rifles and machine-guns crackled incessantly... Our own artillery roared behind us, the shells flying above our heads and bursting everywhere. One could see nothing, understand nothing. With a whirl of smoke and flame before their eyes, and the deafening roar in their ears, the men went blindly on. Odd details only could be distinguished : a destroyed patch of wire, the clod of earth over which one stumbled, Germans standing upright and throwing grenades, a capped officer firing madly... a shot, and he falls, etc.

" Yet one had the impression of being alone. On the right, a few

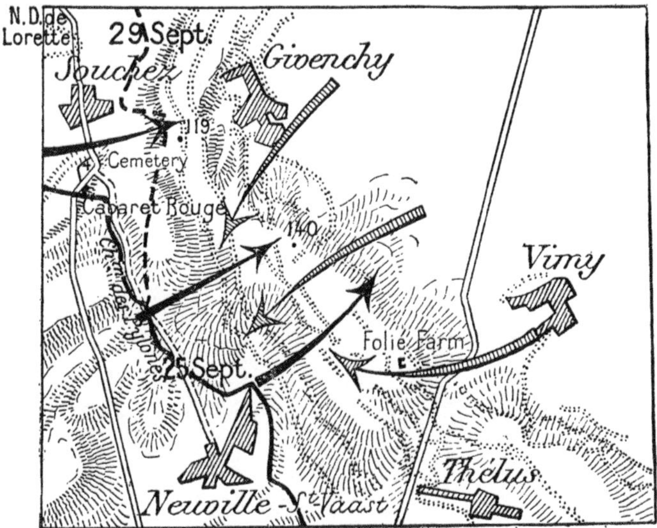

THE ATTACK ON HILL 119 IN SEPTEMBER 1915.
Souchez was taken, but everywhere else the Attack failed.

isolated beings, like one's self ; on the left, three or four *poilus* lying flat in a shell-hole, and firing straight in front of them. Behind, wounded everywhere.

" Souchez village required two more days to conquer. The assailants were held in front of the Cemetery, with very heavy casualties. Further south, the companies which had crossed the bottom of Écouloirs Ravine were unable to hold their ground. Exposed to machine-gun fire on their right, and from the slopes of Hill 119, on their front, their left uncovered, the men, lying flat on their bellies in the mud, crawled back, one by one, over the corpses, to the first enemy line conquered, where the survivors held their ground with great difficulty.

" Evening fell, with the rain still coming down. The trenches were filled with dead and wounded. The attacking battalions were scattered in the shell-holes of the ploughed-up ground. Mud and blood were everywhere " (Captain HUMBERT's *La Division Barbot.*)

The attack was resumed on the following days. Souchez was captured, whilst further to the right, in front of Neuville-St-Vaast, the troops of the 3rd Corps, after crossing a hollow, reached the orchards of Folie Farm. However, the men were extenuated with fatigue, and a violent counter-attack forced them back to their lines.

Fresh attempts on September 28 against Hill 119, by the 60th, 61st, and 57th Battalions of Chasseurs, failed with heavy losses on the crest, in front of the formidable Bremen Trench, whose barbed wire entanglements on the counter-slopes were intact, whilst its machine-guns swept the *glacis*.

Battalions and regiments relieved one another at the foot of the slopes of Hill 119 and along Souchez Ravine, in front of Neuville-St-Vaast — a truly hideous sector, where Death and Mud reigned supreme. " Each night, in front of the Cabaret Rouge, the dead were loaded on carts, while the companies going up the line passed by long rows of other dead awaiting their turn to be removed. "

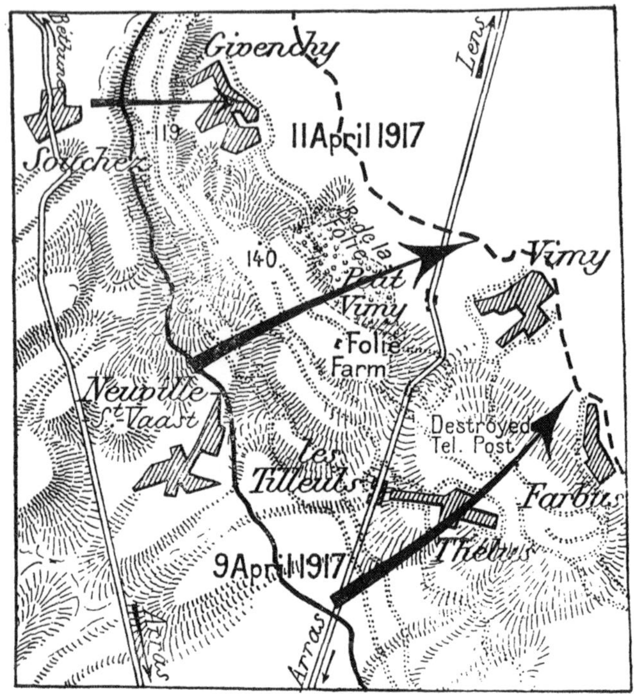

THE BRITISH ATTACK OF APRIL 1917. (*The whole of Vimy Ridge was conquered.*).

The Capture of Vimy Ridge (*April* 1917).

In the Spring of 1916, the British extended their line of trenches towards the Somme, and relieved the French in the sector of Arras, whilst during the following Winter, the front of attack was strengthened and powerfully equipped.

Putting to profit the experience gained at Verdun and on the Somme, more precise methods of attack were adopted, and the material means, especially the artillery, were heavily reinforced.

Vimy Ridge, including Hill 119, was at last to be conquered.

The honour of this arduous task was reserved for the British 1st Army (Horne), more especially the Canadian Corps (Byng), comprising the 1st (Currie), 2nd (Burstall), 3rd (Lipset) and 4th (Watron) Divisions.

The British guns, firing in *rafales* of extreme violence, ploughed up the German defences, the wire entanglements of which were a hundred yards deep in places.

For the first time, the British utilised the indirect fire of thousands of machine-guns which, grouped in batteries, sent a hail of bullets over the German lines. This fire, added to the bombardment, made the revictualling of the enemy impossible.

At dawn, on April 9, a hurricane of shells fell on the enemy's lines and batteries. The number of the British guns was such that, had they been placed in line, their wheels would have touched, along the whole battle-front.

In the early morning mist and rain, red, green and white rockets went up from the German trenches — urgent appeals for protecting barrages and reinforcements. The rain was now falling heavily, accompanied by a violent west wind. At 5.30, the Canadians left their holes, and began to scale the slopes of the ridge. Neither the foul weather, nor the sticky ground affected their fine dash.

In forty minutes, three lines of trenches were carried, and the first objectives: Folie Farm and the hamlet of Les Tilleuls, were conquered.

BRITISH CEMETERY AT THE CABARET ROUGE, ON THE N. 37.

The first wave of assaulting troops established itself on the new positions, the second wave sweeping on and descending the slopes of the ridge. Hill 132 (or Telegraph Hill), then Farbus Village were carried. A number of guns were taken in the village and neighbouring wood. The Germans resisted stoutly in the numerous redoubts on the counter-slopes. Those who had taken refuge in the chalk-pits and in two tunnels, were captured. A desperate counter-attack by enemy reinforcements, to win back the lost positions, spent itself with terrible losses, against the stubborn resistance of the Canadians. The struggle was particularly bitter at the northern end of the crest, held by the 4th Division, and continued with unabated fury throughout the night. The next day, the summit was wrested from the enemy's grip.

The whole ridge was now in the hands of the Canadians, together with some 5,000 prisoners, a hundred officers, 50 guns, 125 machine-guns and a large quantity of material of all kinds.

After visiting Hill 119, *take the N.* 37 *again, at Souchez Cemetery.*

At the second turning (1 *km. from the cross-roads with the stone cross*), *on the left-hand side of the road, used to stand* the **Cabaret Rouge** (*photo p.* 87). Attention is needed to discover, amid the upturned ground, the cellar of this inn, which was transformed into a blockhouse. It

THE CROSSING OF THE N. 37 WITH THE G. C. 49 AT LA TARGETTE.
The car is turning into the G. C. 49, towards Neuville-St-Vaast.

is the last remaining vestige of the place, for ever famous, on account of the furious combats which took place there in 1915.

The N. 37 *continues straight ahead* (*photo p.* 83). On the right, extends a plain which the Germans fortified, between Carency and La Targette, with trenches and strong-points. The chalky parapets of these defences, which were visible to the French, caused the place to become known as the OUVRAGES BLANCS.

To the left of the road rise the western slopes of Vimy Ridge.

Continuing along the N. 37, **La Targette** *is soon reached* (4 *kms. from Souchez*). The place is a shapeless mass of ruins. *Take the road on the left* (*G. C.* 49, *photo above*) to **Neuville-St-Vaast.**

BARRICADE ACROSS THE ROAD AT LA TARGETTE.

NEUVILLE-ST-VAAST IN RUINS.

NEUVILLE-SAINT-VAAST.

Until May 1915, the French first lines were 2 ½ kms. from the western outskirts of Neuville-St-Vaast and 1 ½ kms. from the southern outskirts. On May 9, regiments belonging to two divisions of the 20th corps received orders to carry this strongly fortified village, described by an officer, who took part in the attacks, as "a mass of machine-guns and mine-throwers".

At 10 a.m., the order to attack was given. An hour-and-a-half later, the western and southern oustkirts were reached, four lines of trenches, the village of La Targette and several outlying isolated defences having been carried. (*See map, p.* 94).

TEMPORARY SCHOOL AMONG THE RUINS OF NEUVILLE-ST-VAAST (MARCH 1920).

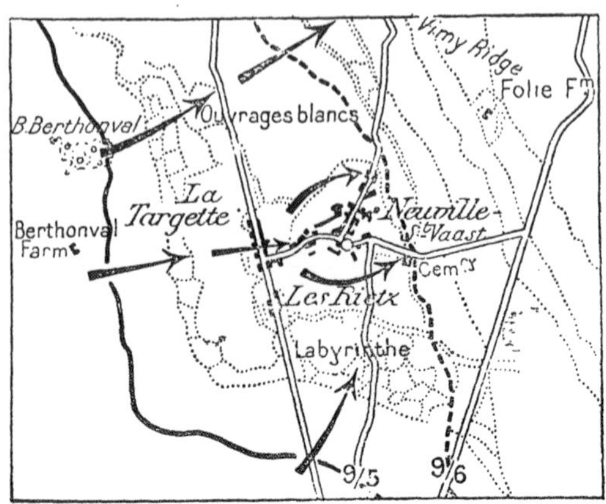

The Capture of Neuville-St-Vaast (May 9 — June 9, 1915).

However, the enemy's resistance increased in proportion as the British penetrated into the village, each house being the scene of a desperate encounter.

During the afternoon, the southern part only of the village could be taken. To the east, the cemetery, where fierce hand-to-hand struggles took place among the shattered graves, was reached. It was twice taken, only to be lost again, the Germans finally remaining masters of it.

On the following days, the fighting continued with unabated fury. No other village in the whole sector had been so powerfully organized as Neuville-St-Vaast. The cellars of all the houses had been reinforced with walls of concrete three to four feet thick, whilst beneath were shelters, proof against the heavy shells, in which the Germans hid themselves during the bombardments. These cellars communicated with one another, and it was thus possible to go underground from one end of the village to the other. Behind loop-holes, level with the ground, machine-guns were posted, and at the cross-roads the houses were flanked with concrete shelters, in which the defenders were locked up with their machine-guns.

On May 15, after five days of uninterrupted fighting, the Germans were driven out of the main quarter of Neuville, although they still remained strongly entrenched in the whole of the northern part and in a few blocks of houses in the west of the village. Their resistance was such that the artillery had literally to pulverise each house. Until June 9, the communiqué mentioned the name of Neuville-St-Vaast each day, telling in laconic phrase of the furious attacks by which, one by one, the last centres of resistance were captured.

Take the G. C. 49 through the entirely destroyed village, to the ruins of the church — a mere heap of débris — *on the left, near the entrance to a street. Turn left into this street to visit,* 1½ *kms further on,* the mine craters on Hill 119, *to the north-east of Neuville-St-Vaast.*

At the exit from the village, there used to be a fork in the road, the left-hand branch of which (G. C. 55) led to Givenchy. It was destroyed by the fighting in 1915, and all traces of it were swept away. Keeping straight ahead, English signboards are soon reached, indicating the position of the mine craters. The largest, known as THE TWINS CRATER (*photo p.* 95), is about 50 yards to the left of the road.

All this district was terribly devastated by the shells. The trenches have fallen in, and are now scarcely distinguishable from the shell-holes. *Although the road continues towards Folie Farm and Petit-Vimy, it was impracticable for cars at the beginning of* 1920.

MINE CRATERS NEAR NEUVILLE-ST-VAAST, *seen from the road to Folie Farm. On the right :* THE TWINS CRATER (*photo below*).

Return to Neuville-St-Vaast, turning to the right, near the ruins of the church, in the direction of La Targette. Outside Neuville, leave the La Targette Road and take the Marœuil road (G. C. 55) on the left. At the junction with the Arras road (N. 37) take the latter on the left.

To the right, inside the angle formed by the National Road and the Marœuil Road, there is a Franco-British cemetery (*photo, p. 96*).

Continue along the N. 37, in the direction of Arras.

MINE CRATERS NEAR NEUVILLE-ST-VAAST.

To the east of the road, in the corn-fields, the Germans had constructed an apparently impregnable system of defences nearly 2 kms. long and extending from the neighbourhood of Ecurie to the defences of Neuville-St-Vaast. This position which, according to a communiqué, was "stronger than many permanent fortifications", gained celebrity under the name of **The Labyrinth.** It was an agglomeration of sacks of earth and cement, forming several miles of trenches and boyaux which, intersecting one another in all directions, led to deep underground shelters. Flanked with concrete redoubts and block-houses, and protected by deep entanglements of barbed wire, the place was defended by guns under cupolas, and by machine-guns placed at intervals of 25 yards.

On May 9, only a footing could be gained in the southern part of the Labyrinth, the artillery preparation having been too short to destroy the defences.

The attack was accordingly stopped, to allow of a new and thorough destruction fire being carried out.

Bit by bit, the Labyrinth was conquered. From May 30 to June 17, the fighting went on uninterruptedly, and was of an extremely desperate character. In a single day, the artillery poured nearly 300,000 shells into the position and its approaches, i. e. nearly as many as were fired by the whole of the German artillery in the Franco-German War of 1870-1871.

Cross the Faubourg St. Catherine, and enter Arras by the Rue de Lens and Rue de Lille.

Franco-British Cemetery near Neuville-St-Vaast, at the crossing of the N. 37 with the G. C. 55.

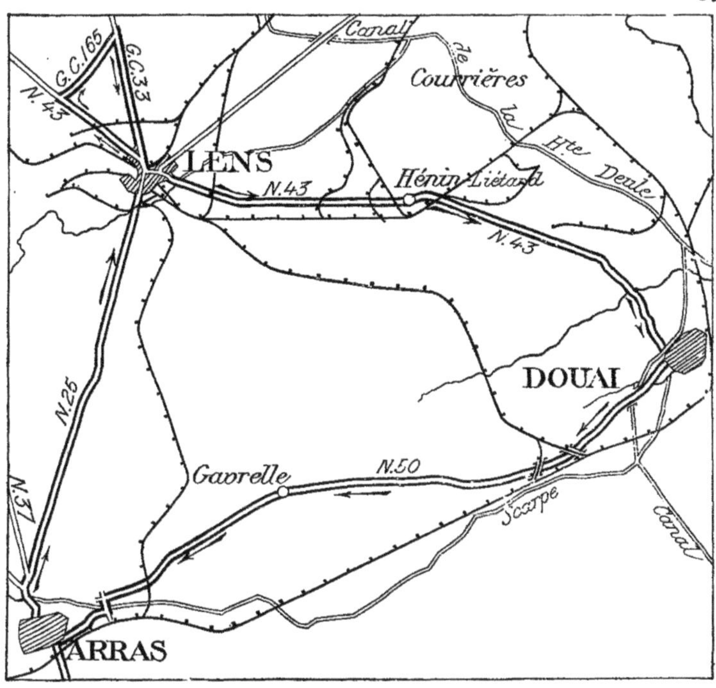

ARRAS - LENS-DOUAI-ARRAS (64 *kms*).

The above itinerary crosses those regions of the north which suffered most during the War. The Germans cut down all the trees, razed

COURRIÈRES.

—

Coal-Pit No. 10.

The Engine-Room, dynamited by the Germans.

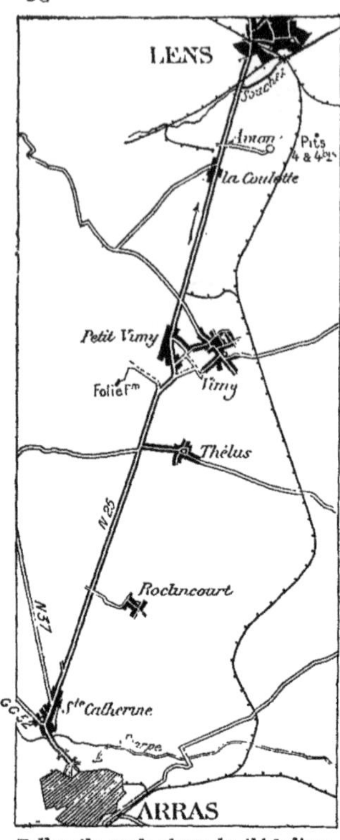

Follow the roads shown by thick lines.

the villages to the ground, destroyed the factories, carried away the machinery, and flooded the mines.

a) **From Arras to Lens** (*map opposite,* 17 *kms.*).

Leave Arras, as per the previous itinerary, but at the fork in St. Catherine, take the National Road which runs due north to Lille. The fine trees which formerly lined the road have been cut down, and small concrete shelters built in the ditches on either side. *Pass* ROCLINCOURT, *on the right.* To the right, massive concrete shelters mark the site of the completely razed village of THÉLUS. *At the crossing with the road leading thither, is a* monument to the memory of the Canadian artillery, *on the right* (*photo below*). Concrete shelters built at the corners of this crossing defended the road. *Further on, to the left, in the fields, is* a British cemetery, with long straight rows of carefully kept graves.

The road climbs up the last crest which dominates the plain of Douai: Vimy Ridge.

Tourists may go to the top of the Ridge and to FOLIE FARM (2 *kms. there and back*), *by taking the earth road* (*the first part of which is sunken*), *which branches off to the left, at the turning in the road.*

MONUMENT TO THE MEMORY OF THE CANADIAN DEAD.
At the crossing of the N. 25 (to Lens) with the G. C. 49 (to Thélus).

THE N. 25, WHERE IT CROSSES VIMY RIDGE.
In the background : Vimy Village ; on the right: Telegraph Hill.

From the road which leads to Vimy Ridge may be seen, on the left, the wooded slopes in which the Germans hollowed out numerous shelters and tunnels. During their brilliant offensive of April 9-10, 1917, the Canadians rounded up a large number of Germans there. On the right begins Telegraph Hill (Hill 132).

The road winds, in descending, and passes in front of **Petit-Vimy**.

In the plain, to the right, can be seen the ruins and temporary sheds of VIMY. From the bottom of the hill may be seen, on the left, the

IN THE RUINS OF PETIT-VIMY, (March 1920).

VIMY IN RUINS.

circle of heights of Hill 119, with GIVENCHY in the background. Hirondelle Wood, scarcely touched, crowns the northern extremity of the Ridge.

The road continues straight ahead to Lens, passing through **La Coulotte.** This advanced position of Lens was the scene of furious fighting between the Canadians and Germans, at the end of April 1917.

On the right, are the ruins of AVION; on the left, Riaumont Woods and the ruins of the numerous *corons* that connected up Liévin with Lens.

Cross the Souchez, then the canal running parallel to it. By opening breaches in the canal banks, the Germans transformed these water-courses into a vast swamp. which protected their defences to the south of Lens.

The tourist enters **Lens** *by the southern suburb.* (*See p an, p.* 109).

LENS LAID WASTE.

LENS.

Originally a county, under the Counts of Flanders, Burgundy, Artois, and the Dukes of Burgundy, Lens belonged to Spain at the end of the 15th century, and was only restored to France by the Treaty of the Pyrenees in 1659.

Before the War, Lens numbered about 35,000 inhabitants, most of whom derived their livelihood from the coal industry. The substratum belongs to the rich coal-fields of Northern Europe, which, beginning near Aix-la-Chapelle and ending to the north of Boulogne, are prolonged on the English side of the Channel. The seat of intense activity, Lens had a yearly output of some three and a half million tons of coal. The very life of the place, which depended almost entirely on the coal mines, ceased at the outbreak of the War. Occupied by the Germans from 1914 to October 2, 1918, the population deserted the city on April 13, 1917.

Lens was literally wiped out. In the Grande Place used to stand the Church of St-Léger, which contained the venerated relics of St. Vulgan, who died in the vicinity, in 570. The base of the tower dated from the 15th century, but the church proper was built in the latter part of the 18th century, and contained some fine wood-work of the same period. A heap of stones and débris now marks the site of the church. The miners' dwelling agglomerations (corons) were razed to the ground.

Great efforts are being made to resussitate the city. Forty-three powerful pumps, requiring a total force of 3,000 H. P., were ordered as early as 1916, and will soon be engaged in clearing the mines. State plans for the building of 500 houses in 1919, 1,500 in 1920, and 2,500 in 1921, have been drawn up. Eventually, Lens will be able to resume her normal industry, but many years must elapse before she can recover her former prosperity.

LENS CHURCH, IN 1918.

The Military Operations around Lens.

Lens was occupied by the Germans in October 1914, after the battles fought around Douai. The enemy enlarged their gains by taking the plateau which dominates Lens to the south-west (Liévin and Angres), and later by the capture of the crests commanding the Plain of Lens : Notre-Dame-de-Lorette and Vimy Ridge.

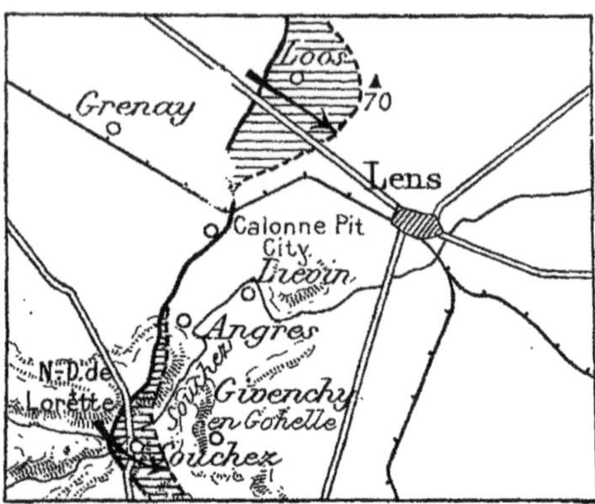

The British Push towards Lens. (Sept. 1915.)

In May 1915, the French seized the spur of Notre-Dame-de-Lorette which dominated the *corons* situated in the Plain of Lens. Prior to September 1915, the front lines ran 1 km. from the western outskirts of Loos, crossed the road and the Béthune-Lens railway from north to south, took in the outskirts of the Cité of Calonne, passing thence in front of Angres through the lowlands of the Buval district.

In September 1915, the British extended their lines as far as the outskirts of the *corons* of Calonne Pit. From here, they could see, rising before them, the smoke from the high chimney-stacks of the Lens coal-mines, which were then being actively exploited by the Germans, who forced the local miners to work for them.

The Lens front was attacked on the 25th by the British and French operating in liaison.

After an intense artillery preparation, the British dashed forward along a 6-mile front.

Several lines of trenches were taken, the attacking troops advancing to within about two miles of Lens. Passing the powerfully fortified village of Loos, the British reached Hill 70, for the possession of which bitter fighting, lasting several days, took place. Reaching the Lens-Béthune Road, their advanced line was now in contact with the German 3rd position.

The British took 3,000 prisoners (including 50 officers), 21 guns and 40 machine-guns.

Many of the inhabitants of Loos were freed from the German yoke, among others, a brave girl : Émilienne Moreau (*see p.* 110).

To the south of this sector, the French captured Souchez, and advanced in the direction of Angres and Givenchy.

The respective lines remained fixed on these new positions throughout the year 1916.

Activities broke out again suddenly, after the German retreat of March 1917. In the following month, the British attacked from Lens to the south-west of Arras, along an 18-mile front.

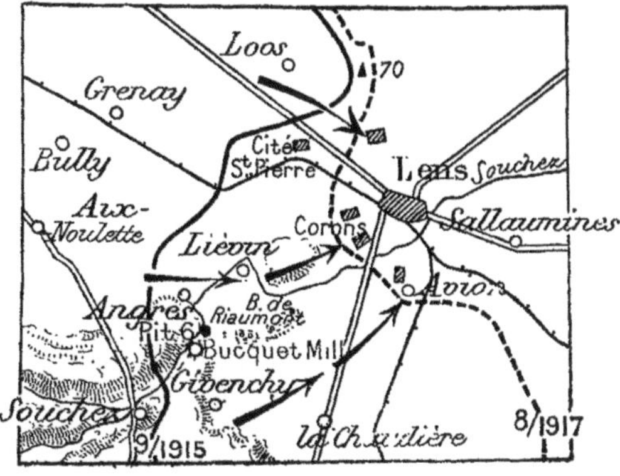

THE BRITISH ATTACKS OF SEPT. 1915— AUG. 1917, TOWARDS LENS.

After the brilliant successes on the Scarpe and the entirely reconquered Vimy Ridge, the action extended to the north-east, in the direction of Lens.

On April 13, Givenchy and Angres fell, whilst the day following, under the increasing pressure of the British, the Germans were compelled to abandon la Chaudière, Pit No. 6, and Bucquet Mill (between Givenchy and Angres), to the south of Avion.

Meanwhile, the salient to the west of Lens was reduced by the capture, first of the double slag-heap, then of Liévin — an important mining centre which, before the war, numbered 25,000 inhabitants. Between Lens and Liévin stretch mining villages or *corons* in an unbroken line. The scene of the fighting was thus advanced to the outer suburbs of Lens.

On the 14th, British units from the south of Loos occupied the Cité St. Pierre.

During the night of April 14, they captured the German defences to the east of Liévin, from Riaumont Wood to the eastern outskirts of the Cité St. Pierre.

A STREET OF LENS, IN 1918.

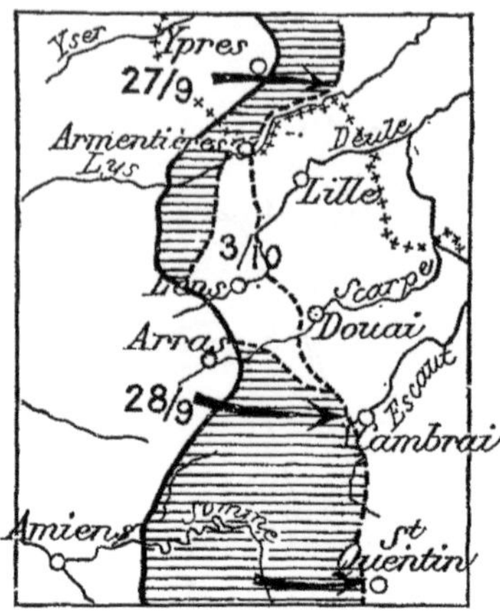

THE ATTACKS FOR LIBERATING LENS.

The methodical investment of Lens continued, giving rise to sanguinary fighting.

The British advanced slowly, capturing the houses one by one, with mines and grenades.

In the meantime, Lens and its suburbs were being steadily wiped out by the shells of the opposing artilleries.

Throughout 1917, the British tightened their grip on the town, by the capture of the numerous *cités* and outlying suburbs.

In the western part of the town, the Germans razed a large number of houses, thereby creating an open space, stretching from north to south, commanded by numerous machine-guns. They also organized the powerful position of Sallaumines, situated on the top of a hill dominating the town on the east, from which numerous batteries of guns pulverized the brick houses of the *corons* (*map, p.* 103).

Then followed the period of the great German Offensives of March-July 1918, during which infantry fighting in this sector slowed down.

On July 18, the Allies' counter-offensives began, following one another uninterruptedly.

The progress made by the British and Belgian Armies, from the north of the Yser to the Lys, the German retreat from the salient to the south of Armentières, and the crossing of the Escaut, before Cambrai, by the British 3rd Army, forced the Germans, on October 3, to evacuate Lens and the dominating position of Sallaumines, under the protection of powerful rear-guards.

THE RUINS OF LENS CHURCH IN 1919.

The Coal-Mines of the Pas-de-Calais during the War.

The basin of the Pas-de-Calais — the centre of which is Lens — forms, with that of the Nord, the coal-fields of Northern France.

From October 1914 to October 1918, half of this coal area remained in the hands of the Germans. The front line here varied but little, and passed west of Lens.

To the west of the town, the destruction caused by the German bombardments was slight in comparison with that wilfully wrought in the occupied area. Here, with the aid of technicians, the enemy carried out methodical destructions with all their native thoroughness, striking at the vital points, and making future reconstruction long, difficult and costly.

The most disastrous destruction of all was the flooding of the pit-shafts. In the Pas-de-Calais, before the coal seam is reached, the shafts descend through some 400 to 500 feet of water-logged ground. To avoid flooding, the shafts are sunk in a special manner, being protected on the inside with a water-tight, cast-iron sleeve strong enough to resist the pressure of the water. Any breach in this protecting iron sleeve would cause the shaft to be flooded. Before evacuating the town, the Germans exploded charges of dynamite in practically every shaft, thereby causing most of them to be flooded.

The German Occupation of the Coal-Fields.

At the outset of the enemy occupation (October 1914), the German troops looted and burnt several of the colliers' *cités*, as well as the offices and warehouses of several companies (Dourges, Drocourt, etc.).

The destruction of the pit-heads situated near the battle-front was carried out by detachments of pioneers, who cut the cables and sent the cages and waggons crashing to the bottom of the shafts. They

THE ENTRANCE TO COAL PIT NO. 2, AT DOURGES, DESTROYED BY THE GERMANS.
The girder-work was dynamited.

GENERAL VIEW OF THE...

also set fire to the buildings. "*We mean to ruin France*", declared the officer in charge of the destructions, to one of the engineers.

The occupation was next "organized" by requisitioning and sending to Germany everything of any industrial value: stocks of wood, coal, general supplies, machinery, tools, electrical plant, copper, etc. The work was carried out by detachments of specialists, sometimes under the direction of civil experts, for instance: chemists took samples of the products made in the factories (benzine, benzol, sulphate of ammonia, etc) for analysis.

In 1915, the Germans ordered a resumption of work in those mines which were not as yet entirely useless, but the output was very limited.

In consequence of the Allies' attacks of 1915, 1916 and 1917, the

COAL EXTRACTING MACHINE AT PIT NO. 1, DROCOURT.
An unexploded charge of explosive is visible in the cavities above the shaft.

By-product Works. Coke Ovens.

...MINES AT DOURGES. (See p. 114).

Germans abandoned the ground, bit by bit, marking their withdrawal by :

The evacuation of the civil population;

The complete destruction of everything that had not previously been destroyed or sent away;

The flooding of all underground installations.

Similar destructions were carried out on a larger scale, previous to their final retreat of September-October 1918.

The expert methods employed were everywhere the same : all props, stays, supports, girders and the like were brought down with charges of explosives ; the drums of the pit winding-machines were blown up with dynamite ; the compressors, fans, pumps, drum-shafts, boilers etc, shared the same fate ; the chimney-stacks were pulled down ; the protecting iron sleeves of the pit shafts was smashed with explosives. The two shafts of Pit No. 8 at Béthune, and Pit No. 9 at

THE WATER-WORKS AND CHIMNEY OF PIT NO. 1, AT DROCOURT.

BY-PRODUCT WORKS OF COAL-PITS NOS. 2 AND 2 *bis*, AT DOURGES,
Blown up by the Germans (*see p.* 114).

Courrières were completely destroyed by the explosion of mines which left enormous craters.

In several places which the Germans had to evacuate in a hurry, the destructions were only partial. On entering, the Allies found notices indicating the points where charges of explosive were to be fired, and the quantity of explosive to be used.

COAL-PIT AND SCREENING INSTALLATION AT DROCOURT, DESTROYED WITH EXPLOSIVES BY THE GERMANS.

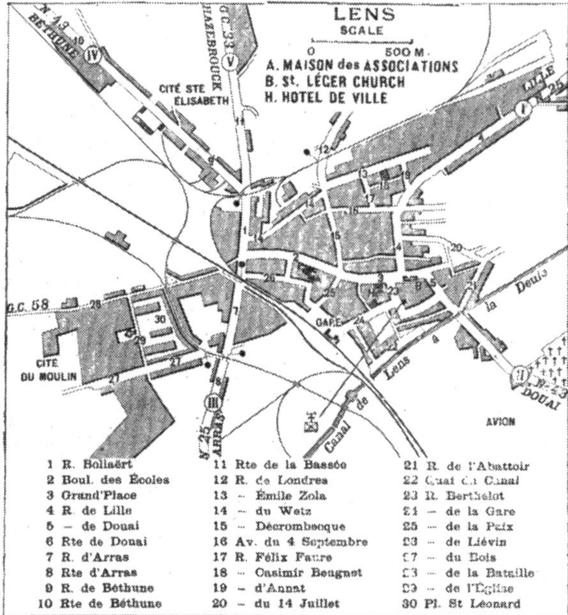

PLAN OF LENS, BEFORE THE WAR.

Note : Tourists coming from Arras by the N. 25 (*p.* 98) *enter Lens* (*p.* 100) *by the Route and Rue d'Arras* (8 *and* 7 *on plan*) *and the Rue Bollaërt* (1 *on plan*).

To visit Loos and Hill 70 (*p.* 110), *take the Rue de Béthune, on the left* (9 *on plan*).

Return to Lens (*p.* 112) *by the Route de la Bassée* (11 *on plan*) *and the Rue Bollaërt* (1 *on plan*). *Take the Boulevard des Ecoles* (2) *on the left, cross the Grand'Place* (3), *turning to the left, beyond the ruined church, into the Rue de Douai* (5) *continued by the N.* 43 *as far as Douai* (*p.* 112).

At Pit No. 7, Courrières, a roll of canvas was found to contain a plan showing which buildings were to be mined, and other documents indicating the quantity of explosives to be used for each operation.

The reconstruction of the mines is a formidable task, entailing the rebuilding of the different plants and the workmen's dwelling-houses, whilst the majority of the mines in the Pas-de-Calais (at Lens, Liévin, Drocourt, Courrières, Carvin, and Meurchin) will have to be pumped out and repaired. This work will require several years to complete.

Lens' War Decoration.

The Croix de la Légion d'Honneur and the Croix de Guerre have been conferred on Lens, with the following mention :

Glorious City, which may be cited as an example of heroism and patriotic faith. Falling into German hands at the beginning of the invasion of 1914, *was in turn, for four years, both witness and stake in a merciless struggle. Organised by the enemy into a formidable defensive stronghold, partially liberated by an Allied Offensive, mutilated and crushed in the course of incessant fighting, never doubted the Country's destiny.*

From Lens to Loos and Hill 70. (*Sketch below, 12 ½ kms*).

On entering Lens, the road from Arras crosses the railway (l. c.). If the level-crossing is closed, a passage under the railway, on the left, may be taken, which leads back to the road.

Continue along the N.25, which becomes the Rue d'Arras and the Rue Bollaërt. At the fork, beyond the temporary Chapelle du Bon-Secours, take the left-hand (Béthune) road (N. 43) which rises towards Hill 69.

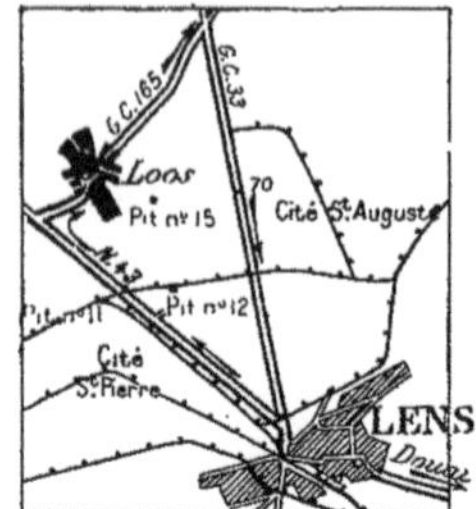

On the right, are the ruins of the Cité St. Auguste; on the left, those of Cité St. Pierre. Beyond is the double slag-heap of Pit No. 11 (*photo below*).

The road descends. Take the first road, on the right, to **Loos** (*G. C.* 165). The great slag-heap of Pit No. 15, with its broken cranes, comes into view.

Loos, a kind of suburb of Lens, shared the latter's fate. A native girl — Émilienne Moreau — received the Croix de Guerre, with mention in the Army Orders, for her brave conduct. The daughter of a miner, she remained at Loos throughout the first part of the occupation, until the first capture of the place by the British in 1915, nursing the British wounded and saving several of them from the German prisons.

Leaving the Church on the left, keep straight along the Hulluch road. 2 ½ kms. further on, the road from Lens to La Bassée (G. C. 33) *is reached, which take on the right.*

Hill 70, which dominates the surrounding country, is soon reached. In September 1915, after taking Loos, the British encountered the formidable positions on Hill 70, which they eventually carried after very hard fighting.

The double slag-heap of Pit No. 11.

Loos, seen from the ruined Church.

A few days later, the sector of Loos was taken over by the French 9th Corps, and held by them throughout the Winter of 1915-1916.

It was on this hill that, in 1648, the great Condé, facing towards Lens, crushed the last remnants of the same redoubtable Spanish infantry which, several years previously, he had beaten at Rocroi.

The road descends to Lens. Stop the car near some deep quarries. It is from here that one obtains the best general view of the extensive ruins of Lens and its suburbs — a striking example of absolute devastation.

In September 1918, the Allies' and enemy lines crossed this hill.

Lens. Temporary Huts and Chapel in the rue Bollaert.

LENS. — SEEN FROM THE RUINS...

From Lens to Douai, via Hénin-Liétard (*sketches, p.* 113, 20 *kms.*).

Returning from Loos and Hill 70, **Lens** *is entered by the Rue Bollaërt. Turn left, into the Boulevard des Ecoles, which leads to the Grand'Place.* The large heap of bricks and stones in the Square is all that the bombardments have left of Lens Church (*photo p.* 104). *Turn to the right, beyond the church, into the Rue de Douai* (*see plan, p.* 109). *Keep straight along the N.* 43 *towards Douai.*

HÉNIN-LIÉTARD CHURCH.

Organisations on Hill 53.

...OF THE CHURCH IN 1919.

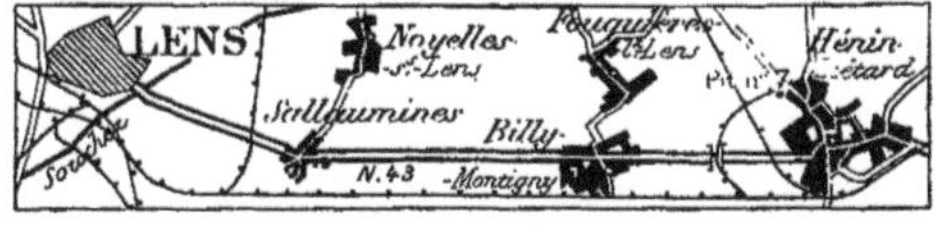

The road rises towards SALLAUMINES CREST, on which the enemy's second line of positions was established. Behind these positions, among the *corons*, are numerous battery emplacements. The road next passes through **Billy-Montigny** and its *corons*. *On reaching* **Hénin-Liétard**, *turn to the left. About* 200 *yards further on, turn to the right, to the Place de l'Eglise. At the church, turn left again, and follow the Douai road.*

After leaving Hénin-Liétard, and 150 *yards beyond the level-crossing, will be seen, to the left of the road,* the buildings of PIT No. 2, belonging to the **Dourges Mines** (*photos p.* 105-108).

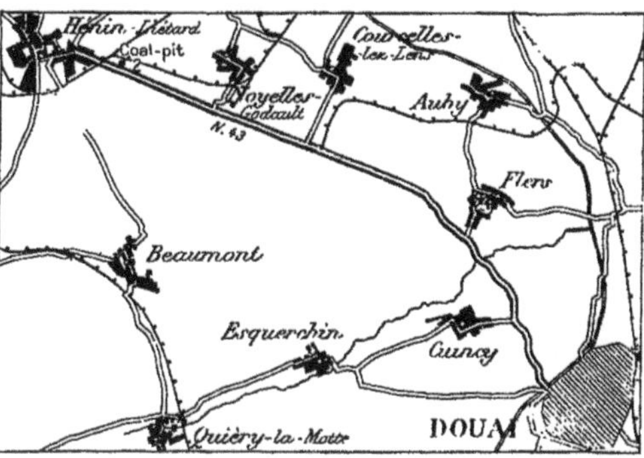

To visit this pit, apply to the Bureaux de la Direction (on the right). Visiting, with a guide, is allowed every afternoon from 1 to 4 o'clock.

Continue along the N. 43 to **Douai.**

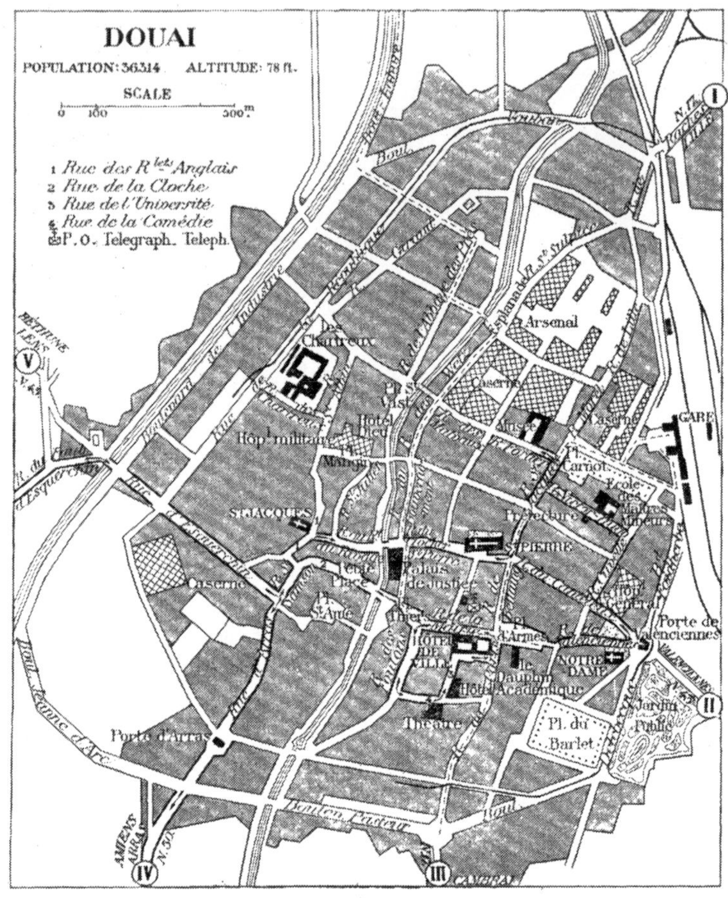

War Decoration of Douai.

Douai was awarded the Croix de la Légion d'Honneur, with the following mention :

City cruelly tried by four years of a merciless occupation. Derived from her patriotism the force to bear all her sufferings, and to prepare, so far as in her lay, for her return to former prosperity.

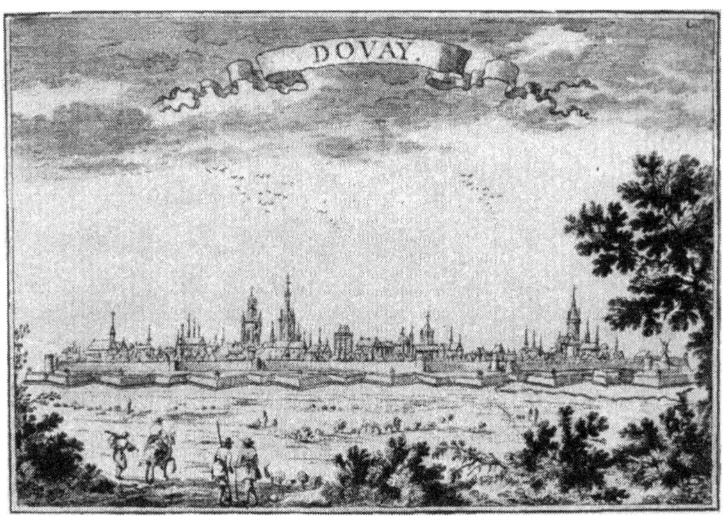

Douai. Old Engraving.

DOUAI.

For centuries a subject of discord, Douai was taken time and again by the Flemish, Spaniards and French, being finally united to France by the Treaty of Utrecht in 1713. To commemorate the town's victorious resistance against Louis XI, in 1479, it was the custom, until the late war, to hold a kind of Carnival each year in July, known as the Fête de Gayant. Gayant, an armed giant warrior of wicker-work, was carried in procession through the town. Douai lost much of its importance in 1887, when its University was transferred to Lille. The city ramparts were pulled down in 1891, but two of the gates — " Arras " and " Valenciennes " — still exist.

This ancient Flemish city gave birth to the following notable persons : Jean Bellegambe, painter, deceased about 1540 ; Jean de Boullongue, sculptor (1524-1608) ; Mme. Desbordes-Valmore, poet (1785-1859) ; the political leaders Calonne (1734-1802) and Martin du Nord (1790-1847). But the most famous of all the natives of Douai was undoubtedly Lesurques, convicted of robbing the Lyons Mail Coach and beheaded in 1796, but as to whose presumed guilt doubts still exist.

Douai during the War.

Throughout the War, Douai was occupied by the Germans. The French Senate reported on the town's fate, as follows :

Here, the pillaging was carried out with even greater thoroughness, if that were possible. The entire population was evacuated, without any regard for the aged and infirm. A judge, 60 years of age, was permitted to use a wheelbarrow, to carry away a few personal effects. Looting began immediately afterwards, and was carried to the last extremes, after which the Germans left the town and bombarded it at short range.

The following notice, which was posted up in Douai on September 2, 1918, at 5 p. m., on the eve of the enemy's withdrawal, proves that the pillaging was organized and executed by order of the German High Command.

There can be no question here of isolated acts of marauding soldiers. It was a veritable enterprise of brigandage, carried out with that thoroughness of which the Germans are so proud.

(Notice posted up in Douai at 5 p. m., September 2, 1918, the day before the Germans withdrew).

In view of the heavy bombardment, the population of Douai will be evacuated.

The entire contents of all the houses are confiscated by the General Kommando.

Specially organized booty companies will collect all articles necessary for the needs of the war, and forward them to the Fatherland, in conformity with orders.

Douai. *The General Kommando*

DOUAI. — EXPLOSION OF A GERMAN MINE ON THE RAILWAY.

President Poincaré, when decorating the City, traced in moving words the events through which it lived from 1914 to 1918.

On August 20, 1914, General d'Amade, Commander-in-Chief of the 81st, 82nd, and 84th Territorial Divisions, gave orders to establish a barrier from Dunkirk to Maubeuge, in an attempt to dam the rising wave of invasion which was threatening you. On the 23rd, enemy patrols were signalled a few kilometres from Douai. It seemed as if the 82nd Division would be able to withstand the attack. Unfortunately, the sector on the right, having suddenly given way in the region of Tournai, the

DOUAI. PRESIDENT POINCARÉ LEAVING THE HÔTEL-DE-VILLE.

troops defending you were compelled to fall back on Arras, and your town, suddenly left without a garrison, without railway, postal or telegraphic communication, and deprived of all resources, experienced a feeling of isolation and abandonment.

You expected immediately to become the prey of the enemy. However, the German Army retarded its occupation of Douai. At first, only rapid incursions and short stays were made, but these sufficed to give you a bitter foretaste of the régime that was menacing you. On September 29, you had the joy of acclaiming the troops of the garrison of Dunkirk, who were seeking to establish a liaison, to the north of the Scarpe, with the Cavalry Corps of General de Mitry, then making dispositions for your defence. But they had scarcely taken up their positions when, attacked by strong columns, they were forced to evacuate the town. That was on October 1. 25,000 civilians had remained in Douai, and they called on France for help. Together, they had witnessed the departure of our troops ; together, they had witnessed their return ; together they had awaited deliverance ; together, they had seen their supreme hopes melt away. Douai fell into the hands of the Germans, and remained four years under their yoke.

Testing-Shop in the Arbel Works.

Gentlemen, as a child, I lived through the occupation of 1870. *It was nothing compared with the one you have sustained. In that other war, the invaded regions were not entirely cut off from the remainder of the country. News from the outside reached us. All circulation was not prohibited. The ways of the occupying troops were hard and haughty, yet, with rare exceptions, they were not barbarous. The inhabitants suffered, but in spite of all, they did not feel themselves torn from the Nation's life. This time, Gentlemen, you have been treated differently. You have been, as it were, enclosed in a tomb, and the stone has been sealed over your heads.*

As your city remained throughout the hostilities within the zone of the military operations, it has constantly been crowded with staffs, officers and troops of all arms, who have seized your houses, relegated you to odd corners, and reduced you to the state of strangers in your own homes.

As time passed, the methods of the occupying troops, far from softening and becoming more humane, increased in grossness and violence. Military perquisitions followed one another in your homes. Irritating requisitions multiplied. The machinery of the factories was carried off. Under a variety of pretexts, the town was constantly laid under contribution to a total of more than thirty millions.

Refusal, delay, hesitation or reserve entailed immediate and terrible reprisals. No matter, you stood firm. And when the Germans ordered you to deliver up your copper and thus compel occupied France to help them manufacture their munitions of war ; when they sought to force the population to do work of a military character, your Mayor, interpreting the public conscience, protested with dignity against this abuse of force.

DESTRUCTION OF THE ARBEL WORKS.

Immediately, fines and arrests were rained on the town. In the dead of night, men were taken by hundreds from their beds and sent to Discipline Battalions, where, by a régime of privations and ill-treatment, it was purposed to break their spirit and force them to work.

At the same time it appeared that, in despair of breaking your will directly, the enemy sought to destroy your mental energy, by undermining your health. As early as January 1, 1915, *you were informed that meat would in future be reserved for the troops, and you were forbidden to touch it. Corn and flour were soon requisitioned, fruit and vegetables were monopolised, poultry and the very bee-hives were seized. The people were restricted to a pitiful ration, and the generous efforts of the Spanish-American Committee were unable to compensate the disastrous effects of this food control. The people were sticken with anæmia, the old folks died, the children wasted away, still your confidence and firmness remained unshaken.*

Night and day, bombs and shells fell in the town, swelling the number of the dead and wounded. Hostages were taken from among you. Your valiant women were sent to Holzminden. Men of all ages were deported to Germany, and others were sent, in the depth of winter, to distant parts of Russia. Some died in captivity, others returned dying from ill-treatment. Yet nothing could shake Douai, or enfeeble your tenacity.

Gentlemen, September 1918 *marked the last and hardest stage of your Calvary. On the* 2nd, *feeling themselves pressed on all sides, the Germans ordered Douai to be evacuated, but took no steps to facilitate the operation. Only the sick and infirm were taken in barges to St. Amand. All other persons had to go on foot, driven along by the soldiers like herds of cattle.*

Scarcely had you left, when organized looting began, and several quarters of the town were set on fire with incendiary pastilles and serpentines.

At the visible approach of final defeat, the Germans gave free play to their pirate instincts. Instantly, everything capable of being transported was carried off, and the rest destroyed where it stood. On October 12, the British 1st Army fought its way into your suburbs. Retarded several days by the inundations spread by the enemy to the north-west, they entered the town on the 17th, only to find it sacked and empty.

A Visit to the Town (*See plan, p. 114*).

Only the pedestals of the monuments remain. The bronze statues in the Place de l'Hérilly (*Jean de Boullongne*) and the Place Thiers were melted down by the Germans, as were most of the statues in the north of France.

The most interesting, i. e. the archæological quarter of Douai is mainly situated on the right bank of the Scarpe, which river divides the town from south to north. On the left bank, practically the only building of interest is the Church of St. Jacques. *To reach same, take the Rue St. Samson, on the left, at the end of the Rue d'Esquerchin, then the first street on the left, and finally the Rue des Récollets-Anglais, on the right.* Built in 1706, the church was enlarged and completed in 1852-1856. Formerly the Church of the Récollets-Anglais (English Franciscan Friars), it contains an interesting 16th century painting of *The Passion.* Over the high-altar, a piece of gilt wood carving, representing *Le Saint-Sacrement de Miracle*, recalls how, in 1252, a consecrated wafer fell down in the Church of St. Amé during the Consecration, and miraculously returned of its own accord to the altar.

DOUAI. CHURCH OF ST. PIERRE AND ANCIENT HOUSE.

Opposite the Church of St. Jacques, take the street which, after crossing the Scarpe, leads to the PALAIS DE JUSTICE, formerly an asylum belonging to the Abbey of Marchiennes. On the right of the façade, a small tierce-point door recalls the original 16th century building, on the site of which the present edifice was erected. The façade, which was rebuilt between 1784 and 1789, is ornamented with allegorical figures of "Justice" and "Truth", between which are the Tables of the Law. Above the windows are sculptured bas-reliefs, the last one of which, on the right, was destroyed by shell-fire.

Going towards the Church of St. Pierre, by the Rue du Clocher-St-Pierre, the tourist passes a block of houses in ruins. Close to a small 16th century wooden house of no particular interest, is a fragment of wall with fine windows — all that remains of the MAISON DES RÉMY, a charming 16th century mansion destroyed during the War (*photos opposite and below*).

The Church of St. Pierre was rebuilt in the 18th century (*photo p. 120*). The vaulting of one of its chapels (that of the Sacré-Cœur) was partly destroyed. Before leaving, the Germans sacked it.

MAISON DES RÉMY, 19, RUE CLOCHER-ST-PIERRE, BEFORE THE WAR.

The fine organ case, dating from 1760, was left behind, but the pipes were smashed to bits with hammers. The débris were found scattered about near the porch, with chasubles, altar cloths, etc., when the town was retaken. The graceful wrought-iron railing round the choir, and several mural paintings in the different chapels are worthy of note. In the Chapel of the Dome, an *Annunciation*, by Eisen, an *Assumption*, by Lagrenée, and several other paintings, have unfortunately been damaged by the damp.

The Rue St. Jacques, on the left, beyond the Church of St. Pierre, leads to the Rue Fortier, in which is the MUSEUM. The three wings of the building look out on a court-yard, ornamented with a small garden. The works of art were removed by the Germans first to Valenciennes, and thence to Brussels. The Allies' victory caused them to be returned. The folding leaves of a triptych, painted by Jean Bellegambe, representing *The Immaculate Conception*, and taken from the Church of St-Jean-en-Ronville, Arras, are of interest. The catalogue contains the names of *Léonard de Vinci*, *Le Guerchin*, *Bellini*, *Le Dominiquin*, *Le Guide*, *Le Bassan*, *Van*

MAISON DES RÉMY, IN 1919.

DOUAI MUSEUM. READY FOR BERLIN.
Interrupted by the Allies, the Germans had to leave these art treasures behind.

Orley, Van der Weyden, Hans Holbein, Rubens, David Teniers and Breughel. The modern painters included *Corot, Courbet, Harpignies and Raffaelli.* The rich and famous library, founded in 1767, contains over 90,000 volumes, including numerous early editions and MSS.

*Return along the Rue Fortier to the Rue St. Jacques; take the same to the right, then turn left into the Rue Victor-Hugo. On the right, at No.*14, *is the* HOTEL PAMART, dating from 1729. *On the left, are the* SCHOOL OF FINE ARTS and *the* SCHOOL OF MASTER-MINERS, both 18th century buildings. The pediment over the entrance and part of the outbuildings of the latter school have fallen down.

Take the Rue François-Cuvelle, then the Rue du Canteleux, on the left, in which is the GENERAL HOSPITAL. The pediment overlooking the street is adorned with a finely carved group of figures. That of the chapel in the court-yard is ornamented with a scroll dating from 1756.

To the right of the General Hospital, in the Boulevard Faidherbe, is the VALENCIENNES GATE (1459). The passage between the towers has been restored. This Gate is a vestige of the ancient ramparts. *Not far from the Valenciennes Gate, and a few yards from the Public Garden, stands the* CATHEDRAL OF NOTRE-DAME. The nave and side-aisles are 13th century, the transept and choir 14th century, whilst the façade dates from the middle of the 19th century. The altar came from the Convent of the Carthusian Friars. A *Christ on the knees of his mother*, attributed to Van Dyck, is on the left-hand side of the choir. The famous ALTAR-PIECE of ANCHIN, carried off, like many of the other works of art, has been returned to its place in the sacristy, where it has so often been admired and studied. The work of Jean Bellegambe, it was ordered by Charles Coguin, Abbot of Anchin (1511-1546). It was removed to Douai during the Revolution

DOUAI. THE HÔTEL DE VILLE AND BELFRY.

and sold piecemeal. Dr Escallier, who bequeathed it to the Cathedral, was able to reconstitute it in its entirety. Consisting of nine panels, several of which are movable, it represents *The Triumph of the Cross* (closed) and *The Triumph of the Trinity* (open). Two hundred and fifty-four figures of apostles and saints are depicted, amid architectural *motifs* of extremely elaborate detail.

The Rue de Valenciennes, opposite the Valenciennes Gate, leads to the Place d'Armes, which was severely damaged (*photos, p.* 124). Before evacuating the town, the Germans mined the whole of this neighbourhood. However, the Hôtel du Dauphin, at No. 16, with its fine wrought-iron balcony, escaped injury, but the other houses, opposite, suffered severely. Of the 18th century house which used to stand at No. 33, nothing remains but a heap of débris.

The HOTEL-DE-VILLE (*photo above*), the entrance to which is in the Rue de la Mairie, on the right (entirely destroyed), has a five-storied belfry, 150 feet high. It is flanked on either side by a symmetrical façade. That on the left dates from 1857-1860; the right-hand one, from the 15th century. There is a large tierce-point door, between two smaller ones, in each façade. The first floor of each façade is pierced with eight windows, between which are canopied niches on pedestals. Of these, the more ancient lost their statues of the Counts of Flanders during the Revolution; the others never had any. In the interior is the Salle de la Rotonde, formerly the Chapel of the Aldermen, access to which is gained by a fine monumental staircase. The vaulting

DOUAI. THE PLACE D'ARMES BEFORE THE WAR.

of this room stands on a fluted monolithic stone column, with spirals, twenty-three feet high.

Follow the Rue de la Mairie, as far as the Place Thiers. There take the Rue des Foulons, on the left, passing some fine old houses: that at No. 14 is in ruins; No. 20, Hôtel de Goy or de la Tramerie, is 17th century; No. 31, Hôtel de Marc du Hem, bailiff of Douai in the 16th century (the façade is of no particular interest). *Turn left, into the Rue de la Comédie, in which stands* the THEATRE. At No. 4 is a fine 18th century house with

DOUAI. THE PLACE D'ARMES IN 1919.

a graceful entrance facing the street. The façade in the court-yard is ornamented with four statues. *Opposite the Theatre begins the Rue de l'Université, at No.* 13 *of which, is* the Hôtel Académique, dating from 1628. The Faculties of Literature and Law were formerly housed here. During the German occupation, the building served as the Head-Quarters of the Spanish-American Revictualling Committee.

On leaving the Rue de l'Université, pass behind the Hôtel de Ville, and take the Rue de Paris on the left, coming out into the Rue de la Mairie again. Take the same to the left, cross the Place Thiers, then the River Scarpe over a temporary bridge. Take the Rue de la Cloche, then the Rue du Samson (on the left) and its continuation, the Rue d'Arras. The latter comes to an end at the ancient ARRAS GATE, which was formerly part of the city ramparts.

c) **From Douai to Arras** (27 *kms*).

Map below (Douai-Gavrelle) and page 126 (Gavrelle-Arras).

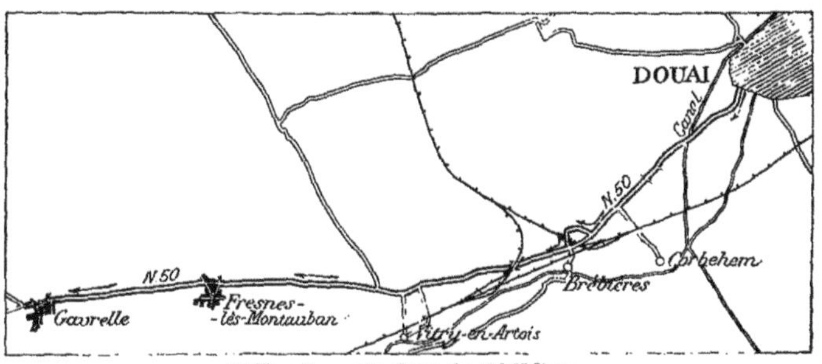

Follow the roads shown by thick lines.

Leave Douai by the Route d'Arras (N. 50) *crossing the* **Canal** *by the temporary bridge. Leave the destroyed village of Corbehem on the left.*
Brébières *(entirely razed) is reached. After passing the ruins of* **Vitry-en-Artois** *and* **Fresnes-lès-Montauban,** *the tourist arrives at* **Gavrelle.**

THE RUINS OF GAVRELLE VILLAGE.

The powerfully fortified village of Gavrelle was carried on April 23, 1917, after a very bitter struggle.

In spite of eight violent counter-attacks in twenty-four hours, during which seven enemy divisions were engaged, the British held their ground.

In March 1918, Gavrelle again fell into German hands, but was

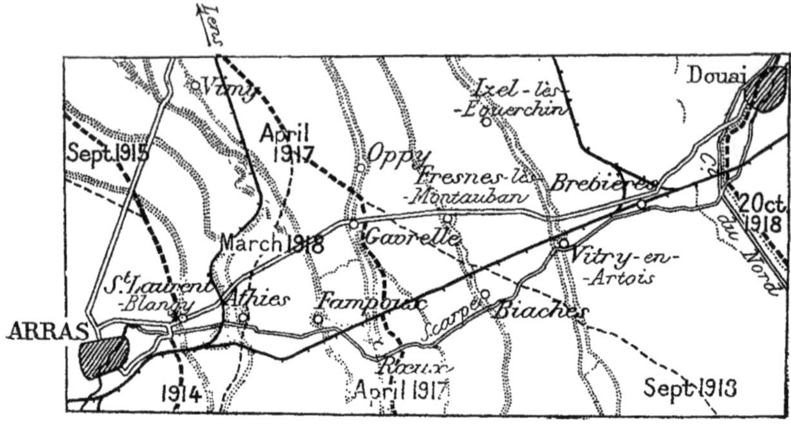

THE GERMAN LINES OF DEFENCE BETWEEN DOUAI AND ARRAS.

finally recaptured on August 26, 1918, by the Canadian Corps of the British 1st Army.

From Douai to Arras, the road crosses all of the many German lines which covered this region and which, together, formed the Hindenburg Line. (*Sketch above.*)

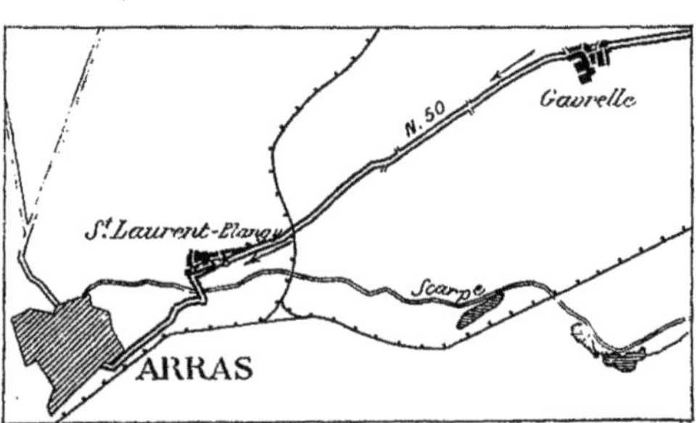

The organization of these famous positions and the battles fought on and around them, are dealt with in the volume: "THE HINDENBURG LINE."

Cross the bridge over the railway, to reach **St-Laurent-Blangy.**

Turn left, cross the Scarpe and the Canal, then right, and so on to **Arras,** *arriving in front of the station.*

LILLE DURING THE OCCUPATION. GERMAN TROOPS PARADING IN THE GRANDE PLACE.
(*Taken from :* **Lille, before and during the War**).

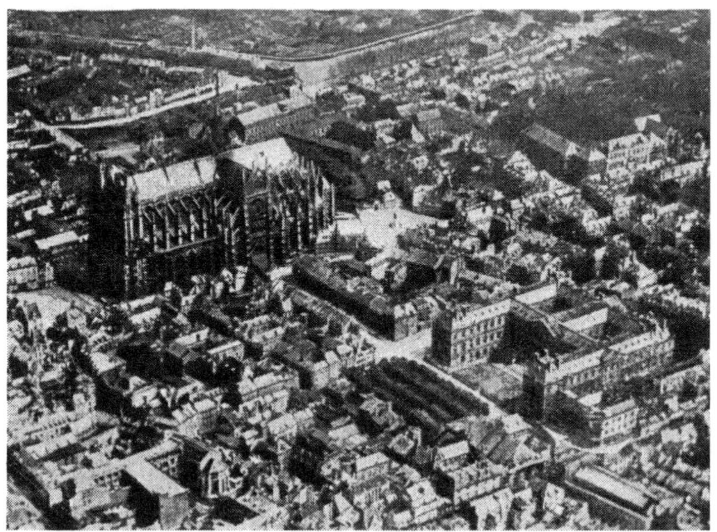

AMIENS CATHEDRAL.

At the bottom of the photo, on the right : the beginning of the Rue Robert-de-Luzarches which, after skirting the Palais de Justice, passes in front of the South Transept of the Cathedral containing the Door of the Gilded Virgin.

(*Taken from :* **Amiens, before and during the War**).

INDEX.

ARRAS. — THE RUINS OF THE HÔTEL-DE-VILLE.

XXX bis 2.138-11-2015

IMP. KAPP, PARIS.

www.ingramcontent.com/pod-product-compliance
Ingram Content Group UK Ltd.
Pitfield, Milton Keynes, MK11 3LW, UK
UKHW041846190726
13854UKWH00002B/742

9 781843 427087